THE MONTREAL CANADIENS

The History and Players behind Hockey's Most Legendary Team

J. Alexander Poulton

First printed in 2006 10 9 8 7 6 5 4 3 2 1
Printed in Canada

The Publisher: OverTime Books is an imprint of Éditions de la Montagne Verte

Library and Archives Canada Cataloguing in Publication

Poulton, J. Alexander (Jay Alexander), 1977-
The Montreal Canadiens: the history and players behind hockey's most legendary team / J. Alexander Poulton.

ISBN-13: 978-1-897277-09-6
ISBN-10: 1-897277-09-1

1. Montreal Canadiens (Hockey team)—History. 2. Montreal Canadiens (Hockey team)—Biography. I. Title.

GV848.M6A43 2006 796.962'640971428 C2006-905319-7

Project Director: J. Alexander Poulton
Cover Image: Courtesy of Getty Images, photo by Bruce Bennett

PC: P5

Dedication

To my father

Contents

Acknowledgments

Writing the history of the Montréal Canadiens is no simple task. I would like to thank all those involved for their patience and understanding in producing this book, which allowed me to squeeze almost 100 years of history into these pages. I would like to thank Colin Burnett, whose knowledge of and passion for Canadiens history knows no parallel. Thanks for keeping me honest!

Introduction

"We don't own the team, really. The public of Montréal, in fact the entire province of Québec, owns the Canadiens. The club is more than a professional sports organization. It's an institution, a way of life."

—Senator Hartland Molson (former Canadiens owner)

Icons. Images. Legends. Portraits of long-gone superstars such as Howie Morenz, Jacques Plante and Maurice Richard line the hallways of the Bell Centre, proudly displaying some of the greatest players to ever wear the *bleu, blanc, rouge* of the Montréal Canadiens.

Le Club de Hockey des Canadiens holds a special place in the history of the game like no other. From 1909 to the present, this little hockey team from Montréal has established a history and tradition recognized and celebrated around the world. The numbers speak for themselves: 24 Stanley Cups, appearances in 31 finals, 10 consecutive appearances in the Cup finals from 1951 to 1960, countless players, coaches and managers in the Hockey Hall of Fame, and one of the best attendance records in the National Hockey League every year.

But what truly separates the history of the Montréal Canadiens from other storied franchises such as the Toronto Maple Leafs is the team's unique connection with its home city and province. From the team's inception in 1909 as the first French Canadian hockey team to today's club, the fortunes of the Montréal Canadiens have followed the rhythm of the city through good times and bad. From early rivalries with Montréal's other clubs, such as the Maroons, to today's tempestuous battles with the Maple Leafs, it is as if the pride and self-esteem of the city and its people are on the line every time *Les Glorieux* step onto the ice.

Nothing better illustrates the connection between the Montréal Canadiens and the city's population than what is commonly referred to as "L'Affaire Richard." Maurice "the Rocket" Richard was without a doubt the most intense and passionate player ever to put on a Montréal Canadiens uniform. On the ice, there was no backing down and no giving up whenever the coach needed the Rocket to score a goal. In the National Hockey League, he was a superstar, but in his home province of Québec, he attained the level of a demigod.

So when National Hockey League president Clarence Campbell suspended the Rocket for the remainder of the 1955 season and that year's playoffs for an on-ice incident in which Richard punched a referee, Montréal fans saw the suspension not only as a slight to the Canadiens, but as a personal attack on Richard by the anglophone aristocrat Campbell, who had never seen eye to eye with the Rocket. The ill will came to a boil when Campbell attended a game between the Canadiens and the Detroit Red Wings just days after Richard's suspension.

Outside the Forum, an angry mob of fans had gathered, holding signs and chanting slogans denouncing the suspension and railing against Campbell with every curse they could think of—in English and French. The hostile atmosphere degenerated further when a tear-gas bomb exploded inside, sending people running for the exits. When the Forum crowd mixed with the mob outside, a full-scale riot ensued.

But the riot was about more than the suspension of the Canadiens' best player; it was about a perceived injustice done to someone who represented the hopes and aspirations of French Québecers, who for a long time were considered second-class citizens. An injustice to Richard was an injustice to all of Québec. Incidentally, without Richard, the Canadiens lost a closely fought Stanley Cup final series against the Red Wings.

The team recovered, however, and with Richard back in the lineup, they went on the longest Stanley Cup winning streak in National Hockey League history, winning five times from 1956 to 1960. Over the years the wins just kept coming, as one Hall of Fame player after another passed through the Canadiens' ranks, giving the team one of the richest winning histories in professional sports. Players like Richard, Jean Béliveau, Guy Lafleur, Ken Dryden and Patrick Roy and coaches like Dick Irvin, Toe Blake and Scotty Bowman all contributed to the team's success. But a large credit is due to team builders Leo Dandurand, Frank Selke and Sam Pollock, who employed some of the most devious and ingenious tactics in hockey history to ensure the winning tradition would continue.

But the Canadiens would hit a brick wall in the early '80s after losing several key players from their 1970s dynasty. Pollock was no longer at the controls, star goalie Dryden decided to pursue a different career, Lafleur began to lose some of his flair for the dramatic, and Bowman could not come to terms with the new management and moved on. The Canadiens were left with few leaders and a highly scrutinized management that made some debatable choices over the next few years. The Habs languished in mediocrity for the first half of the 1980s until general manager Serge Savard brought in several rookies who would put the Canadiens back in the winning column.

One rookie goalie named Patrick Roy would stand well above the rest in the 1986 run for the Stanley Cup and lead the Canadiens to their 23rd championship with his Conn Smythe Trophy–winning performance. With a solid goaltender, the Canadiens stayed near the top of the league for several years, even making the Stanley Cup finals again in 1989, where they would unfortunately lose to the Calgary Flames. The Canadiens would surprise the hockey world again in 1993 as they made their way through the playoffs and to everyone's surprise, beat Wayne Gretzky and the Los Angeles Kings for their 24th and most recent Stanley Cup. After that season, however, things started to go downhill for the Canadiens. Two years later, Roy was traded to the Colorado Avalanche, and the Canadiens lost their biggest advantage on the ice. There also were numerous changes behind the bench and in management, which caused instability on all levels.

There have been a few glimmers of hope in the 10 years since the departure of Roy. In 2006 with Bob Gainey as general manager and Guy Carbonneau as head coach, things looked up for the Canadiens and their fans.

Preface

The Ghosts of the Montréal Canadiens

On March 11, 1937, the body of star Howie Morenz lay at the centre of the same ice that saw his greatest triumphs before the thousands of fans who came to mourn his passing.

The normally loud and energetic Montréal Forum was eerily quiet as an endless line of mourners paid their respects to one of the greatest hockey players to put on a Montréal Canadiens jersey. Many paused before the great athlete and looked around the Forum, reaching back to some vivid memory of watching Morenz streak down the ice for one of his many outstanding goals.

Throughout the ceremony, all that could be heard over the voice of the priest were the quiet sobs of those who could not contain their grief. People who hadn't even known Morenz personally showed a level of compassion that was not equalled until the passing of another Montréal Canadiens legend, Maurice Richard.

With heads bowed in silence, the service came to an end. As people began to file out of the Forum, they talked among themselves of the countless times Morenz electrified the city with his performances on the ice, and how he truly gave the Canadiens the name *Les Glorieux.*

Some of his closest friends commented on his passing after the funeral.

"No one can ever take his place with us," linemate Aurèle Joliat said.

"The news is so shocking, I can hardly credit it," Toronto Maple Leafs owner Conn Smythe said. "I guess the old machine, one of the grandest hearts ever fabricated in a hockey frame, just broke up. He will be missed by hockey men everywhere. To Canadians, it comes as a paralyzing blow."

Howie Morenz was the embodiment of skill and class on the ice. During his tenure with the *bleu, blanc, rouge,* he was the fastest and most talented player in the National Hockey League. In cities like Chicago, Boston, and New York, where hockey had yet to become the institution it is today, fans would come out specifically to see Morenz and once they did, they were hooked on the game for the rest of their lives. But Montréal was his home and where he was most beloved. When the Canadiens traded him to the Chicago Blackhawks in 1934, he was heartbroken at being removed from the city he had given so much of himself to and that had given him just as much in return. After only two short years out of the Canadiens uniform, Montréal management returned him to the team's lineup and brought the smile back to Morenz's face when he put on his number 7 jersey.

But the air of celebration would not last long. On January 28, 1937, during the first period of a game between the Canadiens and the Blackhawks, Morenz dashed after the puck in a corner and was given a rough but legal check by Hawks defenceman Earl Siebert. The only problem was that Morenz's skate blade got caught between the boards and the ice, so when he was hit by Siebert, Morenz's body twisted one way and his leg stayed in the same position. The resulting crack from Morenz's leg breaking in several places could be heard throughout the Forum.

As Morenz sat with his leg in a cast, trapped in a hospital bed, even the many visitors could do little to lift his spirits because the prospect of a future without hockey weighed so heavily on his mind as the days turned into weeks. Soon, doctors began to notice that his physical condition was worsening and he was beginning to fall into a deep depression.

A few days before a Canadiens game, longtime friend and linemate Aurèle Joliat visited Morenz in the hospital to see when his companion was going to join him back on the ice. Before his friend left the room, Morenz wished Joliat luck handling the Maroons in the next game and said, "I'll be all right, I'll be up there watching you in the playoffs." Little did Joliat know that it would be the last time he saw his friend alive.

On March 8, 1937, Howie Morenz's heart could not cope with the pain, and with one final breath, he said goodbye to the world that loved him so much.

Doctors reported the cause of death as a "cardiac deficiency and acute excitement," but those who knew him were certain his death was caused by the knowledge that he would never again play hockey for the Montréal Canadiens and the fans who loved him.

Earl Siebert, the man who unintentionally put Morenz in the hospital, never forgave himself for what happened and spent the rest of his life regretting that game. "I was the guy who killed him," Siebert said. "I was stunned when I heard he'd died. I simply couldn't believe it. He was the greatest all-round player in the game."

Camil DesRoches, writing for the francophone paper *Le Petit Journal,* wrote a few lines that summed up best what Howie Morenz meant to the people of Montréal: "I think the best way to explain it is that to us, the French people, Morenz was French even though he wasn't. It's as simple as that."

Today, his number 7 jersey hangs over centre ice at the Bell Centre beside that of another Canadiens legend and the man who married Morenz's daughter, Bernie "Boom Boom" Geoffrion.

Chapter One

Founding the First French Canadian Franchise

When professional hockey was first established in North America, it was for a long time largely the domain of upper-class anglophones. French Canadians had fallen in love with the game along with the rest of the country but lacked a team to represent their unique contribution to the game.

Since the first hockey leagues were formed, Montréal had several teams competing for fans and the Stanley Cup, but those organizations, including the Montréal Amateur Athletic Association, the Montréal Wanderers, Montréal Shamrocks and the Montréal Victorias, were run by and mostly populated with anglophones. Francophones, long considered second-class citizens, had no hockey team or arena of their own. Hockey was for the old boys club, and they didn't want any new members. So when a young, rich anglophone named J. Ambrose O'Brien arrived on the scene and wanted to form a team of

French Canadians, he met opposition from established teams.

O'Brien had heard of a rift developing in the Eastern Canadian Hockey Association (ECHA) and saw the perfect opportunity to set up a hockey franchise in Montréal. The Montréal Wanderers wanted the right to play home games in their own building, the Jubilee Rink, in the eastern part of the city. The other teams in the league wanted to play in the larger, more profitable Westmount Arena. Wanderers owner P.J. Doran, who just happened to own the Jubilee Rink, refused to co-operate and was summarily kicked out of the ECHA. O'Brien attended the association's next meeting in the hopes of taking the spot vacated by the Wanderers, but he was laughed out of the room for his suggestion because the city of Montréal was already overwhelmed with hockey teams.

At that same meeting was a man named Jimmy Gardner, an executive officer for the Wanderers who had hoped to make ECHA members rethink their decision to remove his team from the new season but failed to move the members in his favour. Storming out of the meeting, Gardner sat down beside O'Brien, who had stuck around in the hopes of getting another chance to convince the board to reconsider. Finding common ground quite easily in their hatred of ECHA members,

Gardner suggested the best way they could get revenge was to set up their own hockey league. On December 4, 1909, a meeting was called in room 129 of Montréal's Windsor Hotel to finalize the formation of a new league, called the National Hockey Association (NHA).

It was announced at the meeting that new franchises had been awarded to five clubs: the Montréal Wanderers, Ontario teams the Cobalt Silver Kings, Haileybury and the Renfrew Creamery Kings, and the new team from Montréal. Naming this new team was a rather easy affair. Since it was to be made up of mainly French Canadian players, it was simply called le Club de Hockey Canadien, or the Montréal Canadiens.

Jack Laviolette, who had many connections in the francophone hockey world, was given the task of assembling players for the Canadiens' first game on January 5, 1910, at the Jubilee Rink against the Cobalt Silver Kings. Once the team was firmly established and the new league was deemed viable, the management of the Canadiens team was to be handed over entirely to French Canadians.

In less than one month, Laviolette had assembled a competitive team. It had two star players in Didier Pitre and Newsy Lalonde, along with Joe Cattarinich, Ed Decary Arthur Bernier, Georges Poulin, Ed Chapleau, Ed Millaire, Noss Chartrand

and Richard Duckett. With the team in place, the Canadiens were ready to hit the ice for their first game.

More than 3000 spectators pushed their way into the Jubilee Rink to witness the Canadiens' first NHA game. Through the heavy layer of cigarette smoke that filled the arena, to the raucous applause of fans, the Canadiens made their first public appearance wearing blue jerseys bearing a white stripe running down their shoulders and across their chests and a large white "C" on the front. White pants and red socks finished off the outfit.

Only 17 minutes into the game, Newsy Lalonde scored the first goal in Montréal Canadiens history and the first for the NHA, as well. Skinner Poulin put in another goal to power the Canadiens ahead 2-0 and before the period was over (there were just two periods at 30 minutes each with a 10-minute break in between), Newsy Lalonde got the crowd on their feet with a beautiful end-to-end rush through the entire opposing team. During the second period the Cobalt Kings came back, but each time they scored, the Canadiens managed to return the favour—much to the delight of their new fans. By the end of the game, the score was tied 6–6. Overtime. In just over five minutes, Canadien Skinner Poulin scored the winning goal. The next day, the *Montréal Gazette* described the Canadiens' victory: "The winning of the match was the signal for a demonstration that recalled old Stanley Cup struggles. The rink was filled with a gathering that gave the Canadiens as loyal support as any hockey team ever received in Montréal." The team was an instant success in the city as people spread the word of the fast-paced, skillful hockey played by the francophone team. Although the Canadiens won only two games that season, they firmly established a place in the hearts and minds of the people of Montréal.

After only one year in existence, the owners of the Montréal Canadiens ran into some legal trouble with Georges Kennedy, who owned a French Canadian hockey team in Montréal's east end called the Club Athlétique Canadien. Kennedy wanted to get his hands on an NHA franchise and threatened to go to court to stop the league from using the name Canadiens, since he had been operating his team before the NHA was formed. Not wanting to go to court and suffer bad press, Kennedy was given the Haileybury Hockey Club franchise to operate as the Canadiens while O'Brien withdrew the 1909–10 Canadiens from the league. But this change in ownership did nothing to stop the excitement and tension that the Canadiens brought to Montréal.

In what would become a common complaint from the Canadiens organization over the years, Kennedy often claimed the league and the referees did everything in their power to make sure the francophone team from Montréal lost their games. After a 5–4 loss against the Wanderers at the Westmount Arena, Kennedy said loudly and clearly for all the reporters to hear that he wanted a francophone referee to shadow the anglophone ones at the rest of the Canadiens games to make sure his team wasn't being cheated. Kennedy endeared himself to the French-speaking population of Montréal even more when he publicly threatened to sue the Canadian Pacific Railway because the Canadiens' equipment did not arrive in time for a game in Renfrew, Ontario.

Although Kennedy was a Montréaler and supporter of the team's francophone identity, he strangely enough changed the Canadiens jersey to solid red with a large green Maple Leaf on the chest and an ornate "C" in the middle of the leaf. It's difficult to imagine a Montréal Canadiens sweater with a Maple Leaf on it, but that did not last long—it was changed back to blue, white and red the following season.

Chapter Two

The First Stanley Cup

When the Canadian Hockey League folded in 1910 because of competition from the new National Hockey Association, the NHA absorbed the Montréal Shamrocks and the Ottawa Senators and saw a few franchise changes when the Cobalt Silver Kings became the Québec Bulldogs and the Renfrew Creamery Kings became the Toronto Blueshirts. But while the league expanded and saw immediate success, the Montréal Canadiens posted several losing seasons.

When the new Pacific Coast Hockey Association (PCHA) opened in western Canada, several of the NHA's top players, including Canadiens star player Newsy Lalonde, packed their bags and signed with the team that offered the most money. Getting a quality player to replace Lalonde was not an easy task for the Canadiens. Since they were not allowed to sign English Canadian players, they were limited to the pool of talent they could find in French Québec. This restriction did not last long, however, because it was deemed unfair to both the Canadiens and to the rest of the league, which equally could not select French Canadian players, and the rule was changed the following season.

Lalonde would return to the Canadiens one year later for the start of the 1912–13 season, but his arrival still could not take the team out of the basement of the league. It wasn't until the 1915–16 season that things began to turn around for the Flying Frenchmen. They finished in first place in the league, and Newsy Lalonde won the scoring title with 31 goals in 24 games. This meant that for the first time in their history, the Canadiens had a chance to challenge for the Stanley Cup, and they faced off against the PCHA champion Portland Rosebuds for hockey's ultimate prize. That season also marked the first time a challenger from the United States was allowed to play for the Stanley Cup.

After not having played in about a month but nonetheless feeling a little weary from the five-day train ride to Montréal, the Portland Rosebuds arrived to face the Canadiens in a best-of-five series to be played at the Westmount Arena. The Canadiens were looking a little depleted themselves, with star Lalonde battling the flu and Jack Laviolette slowed by a broken nose. The National

Hockey Association was hoping that the first American challenger for the Stanley Cup would be a big draw for fans, but because of the increase in ticket prices for the series, only a handful of diehard or rich fans turned out for the opening game of the series.

The lack of fan support and the fact that the Canadiens' two top players were struggling helped the well-rested Rosebuds blank the Canadiens 2–0 in the first game. The Rosebuds' score would have been much higher had it not been for the outstanding goaltending of Canadiens netminder Georges Vézina, who did everything he could to keep his team in the game in what was later described as an amazing acrobatic performance. In the second game, the Canadiens, despite having lost the services of Laviolette and Lalonde because of their worsening conditions, managed to defeat the Rosebuds 2–1 on goals from substitutes Amos Arbour and Skinner Poulin to tie the series.

For those who think violence in hockey is a recent invention, one only has to look at the sport's early games for some brawls that would make recent Todd Bertuzzi and Marty McSorley incidents look tame. These early players might have been gentlemen off the ice, but with their skates strapped on and the Stanley Cup on the line, it was every man for himself. With Lalonde and Laviolette back in the lineup, the Canadiens dominated the third game and frustrated the Rosebuds at every turn—so much so that a bench-clearing brawl occurred when Rosebud player Moose Johnson took a run at Lalonde. When it was painfully clear the referees could not control the barrage of fists and flying sticks, the police were called in to stem the violence and return the game to normal. When all the broken sticks and blood were cleared from the ice, Lalonde and Johnson were thrown out of the game. Losing their best player did not matter for the Canadiens. They went on to win the game in convincing fashion by a score of 6–3. Portland kept the series going with a 6–5 win in game four on the strength of a three-goal performance by Smokey Harris.

By this time, word had spread throughout the city of the hard-fought series, and the Westmount Arena was packed to capacity for the fifth and final game.

The Rosebuds took the early lead, but Skene Ronan of the Canadiens tied the game with a beautiful solo effort, passing through the defence and putting the puck over the catching glove of the Rosebuds goaltender. For most of the game, the play was defensive, because both teams did not want to give the other any opportunities on goal. But all that care and attention to detail did not pay off in the end for the Rosebuds when an innocent-looking shot from Goldie Prodgers from just over 9 metres away beat a surprised Portland goaltender with only a few minutes remaining on the clock.

The atmosphere in the Westmount Arena was electric as fans realized that the Canadiens were about to win the game. The Rosebuds managed a few breaks into the Canadiens' zone, but Vézina turned back every shot they sent his way. When the final second ticked off the clock, the Montréal Canadiens, with a score of 2–1, were the winners of their first Stanley Cup.

For their efforts, each player on the Canadiens team received a $238 bonus after winning the Cup.

Chapter Three

The Early Years of the National Hockey League

When the National Hockey Association disbanded because of internal fighting between managers and the new National Hockey League was formed in 1917, only four NHA teams made the transition: the Ottawa Senators, the Montréal Canadiens, the Toronto Arenas and the Montréal Wanderers.

The new league, already on shaky financial ground, was put in further jeopardy when the Westmount Arena, home of the Wanderers and the Canadiens, burned to the ground in January of 1918. The Wanderers lost all their equipment and could not afford to continue operating the franchise. The cash-strapped Wanderers officially withdrew from NHL league play after only six games. The Canadiens also lost some equipment, but survived by borrowing some from a local team and played the remainder of their games in the Jubilee Rink.

The Québec Bulldogs had withdrawn from the new league in 1917 because of player shortages caused by World War I, and the other teams quickly snapped up their remaining players. The Montréal Canadiens pounced on star forward Joe Malone, who finished the previous season with an incredible 41 goals in 19 games for the Bulldogs.

"Phantom" Joe Malone was so called because of the way he seemed to move right through opposing players with tremendous speed and stick-handling ability. When he was with the Québec Bulldogs, Malone was at the peak of his playing days, leading the league in scoring three years in a row and scoring an incredible 9 goals in one game against a team from Sydney, Nova Scotia, in 1913. He continued his prolific scoring pace when he joined the Canadiens.

In his first season with the Habs, Malone was teamed up with Newsy Lalonde and Didier Pitre to form the most effective line in the Canadiens' short history. In only 20 games, Malone scored a record 44 goals, Lalonde potted 23 goals in 14 games, and Pitre scored 17 in 20 games.

Although the team's fans and management welcomed Malone's arrival to the Canadiens, one player on the team never warmed to the idea. Since the formation of the Montréal Canadiens,

Newsy Lalonde had been the team's undisputed star. Despite leaving the team temporarily in the early years, when he returned, Lalonde was without a doubt the leader and catalyst that propelled the Canadiens to early success. With Malone's arrival, however, the spotlight was taken away from star player and coach Lalonde, who was not a happy Hab. But after Malone pulled himself out of the Canadiens lineup for all away games the next season, Lalonde returned to the number one spot in the hearts and minds of Canadiens fans and management.

After playing the best season of his career with the Canadiens, Malone announced he would only play in the team's home games because he found a job in Québec City he could not pass up. During the early days of professional hockey, it was common for the sport to be a part-time job for many players, who earned only about $800 for the 20-game regular season.

"I had hooked on to a good job in Québec City which promised a secure future, something that hockey couldn't do in those days," Malone recalled years later. "Guys would get injured, and it ended up that they couldn't work. But we kept coming back. Foolish, some might say, but we loved every second of it."

Even without Malone's full services, the Canadiens managed to post a winning record during the 1918–19 season and defeated the Ottawa Senators to win the National Hockey League championship. This victory gave the team the right to face the Pacific Coast Hockey Association champion Seattle Metropolitans for the Stanley Cup.

The only problem was that the Canadiens had to travel to Seattle to play. The world was in the grips of the Spanish influenza epidemic that year, which made it extremely risky for players to stay cooped up on a train for days at a time. Ever the savvy businessman, Canadiens owner Georges Kennedy insured each player for $1000 before the team began the trip out west. Despite the risks, the Canadiens eventually made it to Seattle to play their first game in the best-of-five series on March 19, 1919.

Since the PCHA played under older seven-man hockey rules, games were played alternately under eastern and western rules. Under the western rules, the Canadiens were badly beaten in the first game by a score of 7–0. In the second game, Lalonde came to the rescue of the weary Canadiens and had one of the greatest games of his career, scoring all 4 goals in a 4–2 victory to tie the series. But once again the western hockey rules proved too challenging for the hapless Habs, and Seattle took advantage, putting another 7 goals past a weary-looking Georges Vézina to win game three by a final score of 7–2.

Sky-high scores don't always produce good-quality games; some of the best games ever played in the NHL have been low-scoring affairs of 1–0, 2–1, and even 0–0. In game four of the 1919 finals, fans were treated to one of the best scoreless games in hockey's young history. Both goaltenders put on the finest display of acrobatic saves ever seen on the West Coast to keep their teams' hopes alive. Canadiens netminder Vézina knew that one goal could send his team back to Montréal empty handed, and he stopped every shot the frustrated Metropolitans could send his way.

Eventually, the game was called a draw after an hour and a half of scoreless overtime. During the game, it was noticed that several players looked a little tired and pale, but it wasn't the physical demands of the game that made them look that way—the players were showing the first signs of the dreaded Spanish influenza that was sweeping across the globe, killing millions of people. Now it had arrived directly in the heart of the Stanley Cup playoffs.

In the fifth game, the Canadiens laboured their way to a 4–3 overtime victory to tie the series and force a sixth and deciding game. But things were not looking good for the players on either team. Several had fallen ill, and Canadiens defenceman Joe Hall left the fifth game halfway through and was taken immediately to hospital. In all, five Canadiens caught the virus: Newsy Lalonde, Joe Hall, Bert Corbeau, Louis Berlinquette, Billy Coutu and Jack McDonald. Even team owner Georges Kennedy took ill.

Clearly, the Stanley Cup final could not go on. When it was announced that the series would be cancelled, Kennedy desperately tried to pull together some replacement players to finish out the matchup. The Metropolitans refused and decided that no winner would be announced that year—even if it could have claimed the Stanley Cup on the grounds that Montréal had to forfeit because they could not ice an entire team. The Stanley Cup Trustees decided that the previous winners, the Toronto Arenas, would retain the Cup for another year.

In a telegram to National Hockey League president Frank Calder, PCHA founder Frank Patrick informed him of the progress of the Canadiens players after the series was cancelled. It read:

Frank Calder

All boys except Hall are doing nicely. Hall developed pneumonia today. He is easily the worst case but we are hoping for the best. Have been here myself for three days and everything possible being done. Am leaving for Vancouver tonight.

Frank A. Patrick

After regaining enough strength, the Canadiens boarded a train back east to recover from their Seattle ordeal. Joe Hall remained in hospital because he was still too sick to travel. Just a few days later, despite the efforts of doctors, the 38-year-old defenceman succumbed to the disease. Hall left behind a wife and three children.

Chapter Four

"Les Canadiens Sont Là!" Howie Morenz Revives the Habs

The National Hockey League underwent another change in teams for the 1920–21 season, when the Québec Bulldogs folded and became the Hamilton Tigers.

The Canadiens' Newsy Lalonde returned to the top of the scoring leaders as Joe Malone, who had left the Canadiens in 1919, struggled to find his rhythm with the basement-dwelling Hamilton Tigers. Hot on Lalonde's heels were Cecil "Babe" Dye of the Tigers and Cy Denneny of the Ottawa Senators. Dye was the better goal-scorer of the three, but Lalonde's assists assured him the top position.

It was an exciting race for points until the end of the season, with Lalonde potting 5 goals in a game against Hamilton to pull far ahead and Denneny replying with a flurry of goals of his own, scoring 6 against the Hamilton squad. Lalonde's performance is made even more interesting when you consider that the Canadiens started the first half of the season with just four wins. Despite Lalonde's scoring prowess, the Canadiens failed to make the NHL finals that year as the Ottawa Senators rolled on to their second straight Stanley Cup.

The Canadiens organization was dealt another blow when club owner Georges Kennedy died in his residence on October 19, 1921, at the age of 41. His death was attributed to complications from the Spanish influenza virus that decimated the team during the 1919 Cup finals, from which he never completely recovered. Kennedy had been one of the best promoters in the NHL and was one of the major reasons the Canadiens survived the league's first few lean years.

Upon Kennedy's death, successors were immediately sought to lead the Canadiens organization into the future. Three men, Leo Dandurand, Jos Cattarinich and Louis Letourneau, pooled their resources and put down $11,000 to purchase the team from the Kennedy estate. Dandurand was the organizer, quickly becoming both general manager and coach of the Canadiens. He immediately went about making changes to the team to end its string of mediocre seasons.

Dandurand knew the Canadiens needed some toughness on defence and brought in Sprague Cleghorn from the Ottawa Senators, uniting him with his younger brother Odie, who was already a Canadiens star forward. The brothers' impact was instantly noticed on and off the ice.

Author of *The Trail of the Stanley Cup* Charles Coleman describes one particular game against the Ottawa Senators in 1921 when the brothers made their mark: "In this game, Cleghorn made a shambles of the Ottawa team with some assistance from his brother. A vicious swing at Eddie Gerard cut him over the eye for five stitches. [Frank] Nighbor was charged and in falling damaged his elbow. A butt end for Cy Denneny required several stitches over his eye and more in his nose. This worked out to a match foul and a $15 fine for Sprague. The Ottawa police offered to arrest Sprague and charge him with assault. Lou Marsh, the referee, said he could handle the situation without police interference. Later he wrote in his report that he considered the Cleghorn brothers to be a disgrace to the game of hockey."

Despite the promising 1920–21 season, the Canadiens still needed some scoring talent. Lalonde was no longer the player he had been a few years back, and before the start of the 1922–23 season, Dandurand traded off the long-time Canadiens star.

Since he became general manager, Dandurand had never seen eye to eye with the Canadiens captain, and Lalonde's failure to get along with the Cleghorn brothers proved to be the final straw. Newspapers questioned Dandurand's sanity when it was discovered that he had traded off the biggest star in the Canadiens lineup for an unknown player of considerably smaller stature: Aurèle Joliat from the western league's Saskatoon Crescents.

With Joliat at only 5'7" and 136 pounds, sportswriters had every right to question the motives of Dandurand in trading his star player. But after only one season with Joliat in the Canadiens uniform, they were quick to see the wisdom behind the trade. His size belied an innate toughness, surprising for such a small frame but ideal on the ice. Joliat was as adept at a physical game as he was at the finer skill points.

With Joliat's help and a breakout season from forward Billy Boucher, the Canadiens were back on track, finishing the season in second place, only one point behind the Ottawa Senators. When the Canadiens were eliminated from advancing to the Stanley Cup finals in 1922, many still questioned the wisdom of trading Lalonde; but just one season later, all doubts were put aside with the arrival of another player—one who would change the Montréal Canadiens and hockey history.

Continuing his lucky streak of signing quality players, Dandurand discovered a unique talent languishing in a small-town league in Stratford, Ontario, before the start of the 1923 season. Dandurand received a call from a referee who had just witnessed a young man by the name of Howarth W. Morenz score 9 goals in a playoff game of the Ontario Hockey Association. The referee told Dandurand to come to Stratford immediately before another team discovered this amazing talent.

Dandurand sent Cecil Hart to Stratford as a Canadiens agent armed with $850 and a contract for $2500 to entice the young man. The introverted Morenz was not keen on becoming a professional hockey player, preferring the quiet of small-town life in Stratford to the rhythm of big-city life. He had already turned down several generous offers from the Toronto St. Pats and the Hamilton Tigers, and wasn't about to sign with the Canadiens. But Hart was a shrewd negotiator. He brought the skeptical young man to Montréal and had all the Canadiens players come out to a dinner in his honour. Looking at all the famous faces in front of him, Morenz could no longer refuse and signed with Montréal.

At training camp, Morenz continued to impress the Canadiens brass and was quickly teamed up with top scorers Joliat and Boucher for the first game of the 1923–24 season, against the Ottawa Senators. Morenz scored his first goal in front of 8300 fans in Ottawa in a 3–2 losing effort. Despite the loss, Morenz fell in love with professional hockey.

But the beginning of the Canadiens' season was not going well. At the halfway point of the season, they had won only 4 games out of 13 and sat at the bottom of the league. The added offence on the Morenz line was helping, but something drastic needed to be done to save the season from disaster.

Club owners Catarinich and Letourneau decided to give the players an incentive with the world's greatest motivational tool, cash. With $2000 as a collective reward, the players turned their season around almost immediately and won 9 of 11 games to finish in second place behind defending the Stanley Cup champion Ottawa Senators.

In the NHL finals, Montréal easily defeated the Senators in a two-game total-goal series (the team with the most goals after two games advanced to the Stanley Cup finals). Morenz led the way in the NHL finals, scoring 3 of the team's 5 goals.

In the Stanley Cup finals, Montréal was forced to play against two western teams instead of one as had previously been done because PCHA president Frank Patrick insisted that the

NHL finalist give the Western finalists an equal chance. Montréal acquiesced and still won every game to take home its second Stanley Cup in franchise history and its first in the NHL. The Morenz, Joliat and Boucher line scored 12 of the 14 playoff goals.

The next season, 1924–25, was important for the Montréal Canadiens because it saw the expansion of the league into the United States, providing more competition for hockey's ultimate prize. The season also welcomed into the league one of the Canadiens' greatest rivals, the Montréal Maroons, pushing the number of teams in the NHL to six.

The Canadiens made a triumphant return as champions of the National Hockey League, beating Toronto in the semifinals. They won the finals by default when the Hamilton Tigers went on strike after they felt they were not properly compensated for the new extended season, which featured 30 games instead of 24.

Howie Morenz continued to win over legions of new fans with his blistering speed and spectacular goal-scoring touch, finishing the season with 28 goals and 39 points for fourth place in scoring overall. Unfortunately, the Canadiens would not repeat their previous season's Stanley Cup victory, as the Victoria Cougars of the Western Canadian Hockey League defeated them.

The Canadiens had another bad-luck year in 1925. After a disastrous 1919, with the loss of Joe Hall to the Spanish influenza and Jack Laviolette losing his right foot in a car accident, and the 1921 death of longtime owner Georges Kennedy, now the Canadiens faced an entire season without their top goaltender.

At training camp before the start of the season, teammates began to notice that Vézina looked a little pale and a lot thinner than usual. But Vézina dismissed his friends' concerns and told them he would be in nets for the Canadiens' first game on November 28 against the Pittsburgh Pirates. Before the game, the normally cool netminder looked tired and pale before skating out onto the ice. As the game got under way, fans noticed Vézina wasn't his usual acrobatic and energetic self. Something was wrong. Since Vézina had started with the Habs back in 1910, he had never missed a single regular-season or playoff game.

Vézina would not finish that game against the Pirates. During the first period, he collapsed on the ice and the game had to be delayed while he was carried off by team doctors and taken to the hospital. After a battery of tests, doctors informed Vézina that he had tuberculosis, and that his chances of surviving the disease were slim.

Coming to terms with his fate, Vézina paid one final visit to the Canadiens' dressing room, sat at his locker and wept. He took home the 1924 jersey in which he had won the Cup and spent his final days in his home town of Chicoutimi before passing away peacefully on March 26, 1926. The Canadiens weren't the same without him and finished the season in the basement of the league with only 11 wins in 36 games.

Howie Morenz was now the unchallenged star of the Montréal Canadiens. With new goalie Georges Hainsworth guarding the cage for the Canadiens at the start of the 1926–27 season, the offensive line led by Morenz turned loose on the National Hockey League, dazzling fans in every place the team visited. Cities like Boston and New York, which had given hockey a chilly reception when they first got their franchises, quickly filled their arenas once word got out that Howie Morenz and the Canadiens were coming to town.

The dashing speed and the offensive skill of the Habs' top line was responsible for keeping the smaller-market teams afloat during the '20s and early '30s.

In the fabulous book *Lions in Winter,* by Chrys Goyens and Allan Turowetz, hockey legend King Clancy described the impact Morenz had on hockey during his time: "If you went to a baseball game and saw Babe Ruth power one over the fence, you didn't need to know first base from the a** of your pants to realize you had just seen something special. It was the same thing with Morenz. You didn't need to know the difference between a hockey puck and your belly button to know that when you had watched Morenz play the game, you had seen something special."

Morenz's talent almost certainly would have been the same on any team, but he definitely needed the renown of the Montréal Canadiens to grow into the legend he became while he was playing, a legacy that lasted long after his death. The Canadiens, too, owe a great deal to Morenz, who established a tradition that would breed other Canadiens stars such as Maurice Richard, Jean Béliveau and Guy Lafleur.

Chapter Five

The Dirty '30s

During a time when North America was in the middle of the Depression, the exploits of great hockey men like Howie Morenz lifted the spirits of fans and gave them something to dream about when times were difficult. Adding to the players' mystique was the fact that most people followed hockey through a voice on the radio. The passionate and often exaggerated way the broadcaster described the action on the ice gave players and teams an untouchable, almost mythical aura. Although Howie Morenz was only 5'9", in the imagination of a teenage hockey fan, he played like he was 10 feet tall and made of material not from this Earth. Still, the fans' imaginations weren't that far off.

The Canadiens' top scorer was so highly prized that Leo Dandurand was offered $50,000 from the New York Americans for Morenz's services. But Dandurand knew Morenz was an indispensable part of the Canadiens' success. Trading him would probably have caused a riot in the streets of Montréal because he was so loved by its fans.

Through the 1920s and early '30s, the legend of Howie Morenz and the Canadiens grew to amazing proportions as he scored his way into the record books by amassing the first-ever 50-point season and leading the Canadiens to two consecutive Stanley Cups in 1930 and 1931.

The Canadiens would need all the talent they could get in the Cup finals of 1930, facing some of the toughest competition for hockey's ultimate prize. They had finished the regular season tied for first place with the Montréal Maroons and were in for a tough playoff start against the Chicago Blackhawks in a two-game total-goal series. Goalie Georges Hainsworth did the job for the Habs in the first game, shutting out the Hawks in a defensive 1–0 matchup. In the second game, the Blackhawks managed to put two goals by Hainsworth, but the Canadiens were able to score one goal to tie the total goals at 2 apiece. With the game score set at 2–1, three overtime periods were required before Morenz came to the rescue with a goal, sending the Montréal Forum crowd into a frenzy.

The team had an equally difficult time with the New York Rangers in the semifinals, going into a fourth overtime period before the first game was ended on a goal by Canadiens forward

Gus Rivers. Hainsworth was the story in the second game as he shut out the Rangers with a series-ending 2–0 victory, advancing his team to the finals against the defending Stanley Cup champion Boston Bruins.

For the past three years, the Bruins had been one of the best teams in the NHL, leading the league in points twice and winning the Stanley Cup in 1929 for the first time in franchise history. With scoring talent like Cooney Weiland and Dit Clapper on the rush and the solid defence of Eddie Shore protecting the line, defeating the Bruins was no easy task for the Canadiens. But the Canadiens were on fire in the playoffs and the goaltending performance of Hainsworth once again saved the day in game one, when he shut out the Bruins in a surprise 3–0 victory.

In the second game, the Canadiens had a little more resistance from the Bruins, who did not want to let the Canadiens walk away with the Cup. It was a tight checking game that had the crowd at the Montréal Forum on their feet cheering for their team to bring home the Cup. Every time Morenz got the puck on his stick, you could hear the crowd begin to wind up their favourite song as Morenz streaked down the ice: *"Les Canadiens sont là!"*

The Canadiens came out quickly, jumping to an early lead of 3–0 before Boston's Eddie Shore rushed the length of the ice and put the Bruins back in the game. The Bruins had the Canadiens running around in circles and before the Habs could figure out how to break through, Boston scored 2 more goals to tie it up.

But the Canadiens had an answer. When Nick Wasnie put them in the lead late in the third period, the roof of the Forum nearly lifted off the building because the crowd cheered so loudly. In the remaining minutes of the game, Boston scoring ace Cooney Weiland rushed to the front of the net to get the rebound of a slap shot from the point. He kicked the puck in with his skate in desperation, but the goal was disallowed.

Hainsworth held the fort for the rest of the game, and the Canadiens celebrated the third Stanley Cup victory in their history and a second for their star player, Morenz. Hainsworth was the story of the finals, recording three shutouts and an incredible 0.75 goals against average in the entire playoffs, a record that to this day has not been equalled.

Montréal finished the 1930–31 season just behind the Bruins, and in that year's semifinals, the two teams faced off in a rematch of the previous season's Stanley Cup matchup.

It took them five games, but the Canadiens emerged as the winners to crush Boston's hopes yet again. The Habs continued playing solid hockey in the finals and beat the Chicago Blackhawks in game five to take home their second consecutive Stanley Cup.

In 1931–32, the Canadiens would have another successful regular season, finishing first in the league, but they were taken out prematurely by a strong New York Rangers squad in the first round. Still, the Canadiens and their fans felt confident they could carry their success through into the next season.

But the Morenz era had seen its peak. The "Stratford Streak" had been in the league nearly a decade and was beginning to show signs of age. Although still as popular with the fans as he was during his prime, Morenz had begun to lose his touch, and for the first time in a long time, he was completely out of the scoring race by the end of the 1934 regular season. The Montréal Canadiens were eliminated once again during the first round of the playoffs, this time by the Chicago Blackhawks.

Looking past the popular conception that the Canadiens have always been a successful team, you will find a period between 1932 and 1943 where the Habs often sat at the bottom of the league and struggled each season to make the playoffs.

Canadiens fans realized that all was not well with their team when before the start of the 1934–35 season, Dandurand traded their greatest asset to the Chicago Blackhawks. Montréal fans have always demanded success from their team's players, and even the great Howie Morenz was not immune from the Forum boo birds. After so many years of leading the Canadiens in scoring, the fans had come to expect a certain performance from Morenz, and when he only managed to score 8 goals and 13 assists in 1933–34 regular season, he was booed regularly for his lack of production. Rumours of a trade circulated over the summer, as they regularly do in hockey. Even the man himself did not deny that a trade could happen, given his lack of scoring and frequent injuries over the previous two years. Still, Canadiens fans refused to believe Morenz would be traded, even though he was often the target of their frustrations.

However, just before the start of the 1934 NHL season, Habs fans opened up their morning newspapers to find that their beloved Howie Morenz had been traded along with goaltender Lorne Chabot to the Blackhawks in return for three players (who, incidentally, only lasted one year with the Habs). Before the players left for the Blackhawks training camp, Canadiens management organized a farewell dinner in Morenz's honour. Before the evening began, Dandurand stood before all the players and their friends and family and toasted the Canadiens (and now Hawks) forward: "As long as I am associated with the Canadiens, no other player will ever wear the number seven jersey of Howie Morenz."

After playing two less-than-spectacular seasons with the Chicago Blackhawks and the New York Rangers, Morenz wanted to return to Montréal to end his career with the team that had given him so much. Dandurand traded off two minor players to get Morenz back for the start of the 1936–37 season. Fans at the Forum gave Morenz a deafening round of applause when he hit the ice for the first home game of the season, happy to see the old "Stratford Streak" back in a Canadiens uniform where he belonged. But the aging superstar had lost his touch and only managed to score 4 goals in 30 games. His last game was played on January 28, 1937, against the Blackhawks. He broke his leg in a collision with Chicago defenceman Earl Siebert and never again left the hospital. Morenz died in a Montréal hospital on March 8, 1937, of what doctors suspected was a pulmonary embolism.

After Morenz's death, fans seemed to lose faith in the Canadiens. For the next few years, they played before crowds as small as 3000, and the team failed to renew fans' faith until another superstar came along.

Chapter Six

The Montréal Maroons Rivalry

Without Morenz, the Canadiens continued to struggle to win games and make it anywhere past the first round of the playoffs. But Montréal was not completely devoid of hockey excitement during this period. Leo Dandurand was first and foremost an excellent promoter. In 1924, he had helped a group of business owners obtain the Montréal Maroons franchise to represent the other side of the city's two solitudes. It was the perfect drawing card for Montréal in a time when hockey was having difficulty staying in business in other cities. He knew that there was no better rivalry than the natural one that existed between anglophones and francophones in the city, so why not put two teams on the ice that represented both sides? And it worked!

The *Montréal Gazette* described the situation perfectly when it was announced in the fall of 1924 that Montréal would be granted another franchise: "Montréal will have two teams. One French-Canadian and one British-Canadian!"

Today, most Montréal Canadiens fans are keenly aware of their team's rivalry with the Toronto Maple Leafs, but during the '20s and '30s, there was no greater animosity on and off the ice than a game played at the Forum between the Maroons and the Canadiens. From the outset, these were two teams that did not care for the other one bit.

Regular games were filled with high sticks, curse words, bloody noses, and the occasional fight, but when games meant something more to either team, it was downright warfare—for the fans as much as for the players.

On many a night at the Forum when the Canadiens were playing the Maroons, fans would arrive early and engage in verbal bouts before the teams even took to the ice. At that time, most seats were general admission, so ushers would crowd in as many people as they could on big nights, making an already tense atmosphere even more so. People pushed, shoved, cursed, and fought about everything and anything. Things were equally tense down on the ice.

Players knew there was more to these games than simple bragging rights. Every goal was important and players fought like their careers depended on it each minute they were on the ice.

During one game against the Maroons, Canadien Aurèle Joliat led a forward rush into the Maroons zone late in the first period with no score on the board. With Clint Benedict in nets for the Maroons, goals were hard to come by, so every single chance on net got Canadiens supporters on their feet. Joliat led Montréal's attack into the zone and fired a shot into Benedict's feet. The goalie kicked the puck back out, but Joliat was certain it had just crossed the line. When the goal judge didn't signal a goal, Joliat went berserk.

Goal judges at the time were shielded from the crowd by a protective cage, but from the ice, players could get at them simply by going over the boards. Joliat and teammate Billy Boucher attacked the goal judge with their sticks while a fan had managed to open the cage from the other side and began to rain blows down on the defenseless official. As security removed the fan from the cage and Joliat and Boucher regained their senses, Maroons star forward Nels Stewart grabbed the loose puck after referees failed to stop the play, skated up the ice and scored. Maroons fans were enraged that no penalties were given to Boucher or Joliat, while Canadiens fans were livid that the play hadn't been stopped. Police had their hands full stopping all the fights that continued to flare up throughout the intermission.

Many of the fights that broke out during these games weren't even about hockey. Often, it was a strange mix of fan support based on language affiliation.

But the rivalry did not last long. By 1938, the Maroons no longer had the drawing power of their cross-town rivals, the Canadiens. The Maroons were left without stars because of the retirement of players like Lionel Conacher and goaltender Alex Connell. The fiery King Clancy, who had been a star for the Ottawa Senators and the Toronto Maple Leafs, was brought in as coach to revive the players, but nothing could be done to save the team from its fate. With the threat of war on the horizon, the economics and simple logistics of running a competitive team in a city with two franchises proved too much for Maroons owners. They decided to suspend operations for one year to see if they could come back in 1940, but then decided it wasn't good business to do so.

The Montréal Canadiens had lost their greatest rival, and the NHL would not see such animosity between two teams until the late '40s, '50s, and '60s matchups between the Habs and the Maple Leafs. But that rivalry still can never compare to the intensity with which the Canadiens and the Maroons battled it out like squabbling siblings for 14 years.

Chapter Seven

The Arrival of "the Rocket"

By 1939, things were looking bleak for the Canadiens. They finished the 1939–40 season at the bottom of the league, with only 10 wins in 48 games. Boston was back on top, but the New York Rangers took home the Cup after a thrilling final versus the Toronto Maple Leafs. The lone bright spot for the Habs was the play of Hector "Toe" Blake, who finished the season among the top-10 scoring leaders. Something had to be done to shake the Canadiens out of their losing ways and bring the Forum back to life.

Before the start of the 1940–41 season, Tommy Gorman was brought on as general manager and Dick Irvin was coaxed out of his Toronto coaching job to take over the desperate Canadiens. It wasn't before long things began to shift in the team's favour with the addition of a few key players who would eventually lead the Habs back to glory.

The first key ingredient in establishing the successful future of the Canadiens was the signing of forward Elmer Lach and the solid defensive skills of Émile "Butch" Bouchard and Ken Reardon. But even with this injection of talent, the Canadiens only managed to pull themselves out of the basement of the league a few points ahead of the pitiful Brooklyn Americans. It wasn't until the arrival of a quiet kid from the Bordeaux area of Montréal that things started to turn around for the Canadiens.

The scouting reports on Maurice Richard all said the same thing. He was an excellent player with much potential, but he was just too fragile to play in the National Hockey League. Playing with the amateur Senior Canadiens, Richard broke his ankle and spent a complete season watching from the sidelines. In his second year with the Senior Canadiens, he broke his wrist and had lost all hope of making it into the professional ranks. But Dick Irvin saw something in the young, fiery Richard and invited him to the Canadiens training camp to try out for the team. Irvin recognized the potential in Richard, who possessed an incredible shot and amazing speed but needed to develop some toughness before he could crack the Canadiens squad. Irvin decided to give the rookie a test.

To see if Richard had what it took to survive in the NHL with the tough guys, Irvin told resident enforcer Murph Chamberlain to test the rookie's mettle. With a simple, "Understood, coach!" Chamberlain took a run at Richard and knocked him into the boards. Richard fell hard, but rebounded so fast that Chamberlain didn't have a chance to get away before Richard was on top of him with fists flying. It took three players to remove Richard from his teammate, and with that incident, Irvin knew the scouting reports were wrong and that the kid had what it took to play for the Montréal Canadiens.

Although he broke his ankle only 15 games into his rookie season, Richard earned himself a spot on the team despite the questions surrounding his health. He returned to the lineup for the 1943–44 season and was teamed with Elmer Lach and Toe Blake to form one of the greatest trios to play the game, nicknamed the Punch Line.

Just before the beginning of the new season, Richard's wife gave birth to their first child, Huguette, who weighed 9 pounds at birth. Richard, who wore the number 15 during his first year, asked if he could change his number to 9 in honour of his daughter.

That year marked a remarkable turnaround for the Canadiens. With the players in good shape and the solid goaltending of Bill Durnan, the team started the season with 14 straight wins. Montréal fans and media also were becoming well aware of the young right winger, who quickly earned the nickname "Rocket" because of his tremendous speed on the ice.

Right from the start, Maurice Richard was a favourite of the tough Montréal Forum crowd. Phil Watson, who played for the Canadiens during the 1943–44 season, described how fans welcomed their new star player at the Forum in Dick Irvin's book *The Habs*: "One thing I remember is that all those French people in Montréal, they all thought he was the greatest thing from the start. To give you an example, if Elmer Lach scored a goal the guy would announce, "Goal by Elmer Lach." Then Toe Blake would get one and the guy would say, "Goal by Toe Blake." But when it came to Maurice Richard, the guy would start yelling, "Goal scored by MAUUREEEEECE REEEEECHAAAAARD!!!!!"

Montréal fans knew they had a special player on their team when during the 1944 playoffs, Richard scored all 5 goals in a 5–1 win over the Toronto Maple Leafs. The next day, papers across the city, English and French, printed the headline: "Richard 5, Toronto 1!" Montréal was the hands-down favourite to win the Cup that year, because as the team had only lost five games all season. The predictions were right, as the team crushed the hapless Leafs, winning the final game of the series by a score of 11–0. The Habs rolled on into the finals for the first time in 13 years and easily beat the Chicago Blackhawks to win the Stanley Cup. Richard led the team in scoring for the playoffs with 12 goals and was the obvious favourite of the fans despite the excellent work of the team as a whole.

In the 1944–45 season, Maurice Richard put forward an incredible performance that would establish him as one of the all-time greats in the hockey world and make him a certifiable legend in Montréal.

During that season, on December 29, 1944, he had to move his new family to a bigger apartment the same night he had a game against the Detroit Red Wings. After a full day of lifting heavy furniture, Richard made his way down to the Forum before the start of the game and told his teammates he would not be much help to them after the backbreaking work. But despite his sore muscles, Richard went out and scored 5 goals and assisted on 3 others.

About one month later, he scored one of his most memorable goals against that same Red Wings team on February 3, 1945, one that would lift him to a status on par with another great Canadien, Howie Morenz.

"Over the years, people have asked me whether it was true that I actually scored a goal while carrying an opponent on my back, and the answer is, yes!" Richard once said looking back on that amazing night against Detroit.

During the play in question, Richard had taken control of the puck and was making his way through the neutral zone when he noticed he had only one player left to beat before having an open path to the Detroit net. That one player was all-star defenceman Earl Seibert. As Seibert cut across the ice, he realized he could not get in front of Richard, who had come at him in full flight, so he did the only thing he could think of to stop the Rocket. As Richard was about to break to the net, Seibert wrapped his arms around Richard's shoulder and tried to drag him down to the ice, but Richard just dug his skates in deeper and pressed on toward his goal like a man possessed. In desperation, Seibert then jumped right on Richard's back, trying to use his 200-pound frame to take him down. Forum fans were awestruck as they heard the sound of Richard's skates digging into the ice from the extra burden as he continued toward the net. Despite the burning in his legs, Richard never gave up, and the crowd loved him for it. Nothing was going to keep him from scoring.

Richard best described the incredible event to the throng of reporters that surrounded him in the dressing room after the game: "I felt his skates lifting off the ice and flying up in the air. I think he weighed about 200 pounds. I felt as if I might cave in. The goaltender moved straight out for me, and somehow I managed to jab the puck between his legs while Seibert kept riding my back!"

As the spectacular goals kept coming that season, Richard was slowly inching his way to a record that no one thought could be equalled or broken. Montréal Canadiens superstar Joe Malone established a record of 44 goals in an incredible 20 games in 1917, his first year in the National Hockey League. That record became the benchmark all snipers in the league aspired to but never thought they could beat. As the NHL expanded and the season grew to 50 games, it became more and more of a possibility, but still, many thought the magic mark of 50 goals in 50 games could never be reached. That was, until Maurice Richard came along.

With his talent for the dramatic, Richard scored his record-breaking 45th goal against the Toronto Maple Leafs as the clock ticked away late in the third period and former record-breaker Joe Malone watched from his seat in the Forum. Throughout the game, Richard was shadowed relentlessly by a Toronto team that did not want to be remembered for giving up the record-breaking goal. But the Rocket could not be kept in check all game. With only three minutes left in the third period, Toe Blake caught Richard with a pass in behind the defence and the Rocket found himself one on one with Toronto goaltender Frank McCool. Trying to anticipate the shot, McCool attempted to cut down the angle, but Richard shot the puck into the right corner for his 45th goal. The Forum erupted while McCool hung his head and quietly retrieved the puck from the net.

After the game, quote-hungry reporters swarmed Richard, looking for something juicy to put in their leads. Well aware that the crowds at the Forum were the inspiration for his amazing feats, Richard paused when asked by one anglophone reporter if he wanted to dedicate his achievement to anyone in particular, then simply answered: "This record honours all French-Canadians." From that point, Maurice Richard became a legend in the province of Québec.

His next record came in the last game of the season against the Boston Bruins. With 49 goals to his name, Richard needed just one more to make history. All game, Boston fans held their breaths every time Richard got his hands on the puck, but after almost three full periods, he had yet to score. Just a few minutes before the end of the game, linemates Lach and Blake tried everything they could to get the puck to Richard. With just two minutes left on the clock, Richard and Lach rushed into the Bruins zone. Lach cut across in front of the net with the puck, trying to get as many players as possible to follow him before passing to Richard, but he ran into a Bruins defenceman and the puck was lost under a scramble of players. Somehow, in the jumble of arms and legs, Richard managed to find the puck and shovel it into the net for his 50th goal.

Bruins goaltender Harvey Bennett immediately protested to the referee that he had been interfered with, but the referee did not see any infraction and the goal stood. Richard and Lach jumped into the air, catching each other, while the Bruins looked on in disappointment. Back in Montréal, fans crowed into the Windsor Train Station and gave the Rocket a hero's welcome when he arrived, surprising the shy, quiet Richard.

After that feat, those who dismissed Richard as a flash in the pan were rethinking their assessment.

"I tried to size him up, but I couldn't," said Toronto Maple Leafs goaltender Johnny Bower, who faced more than his share of Richard shots. "He'd score on me through my legs, then another along the ice, then on one side and then on the other side. He had me going crazy. The biggest thrill of my life was when he retired."

With records falling beneath the blade of his stick, Maurice Richard drew a lot of attention from the tougher players around the league who would try everything to provoke his fiery character. But with each incident, his popularity with the people of Québec grew stronger—to the point where, in their eyes, he could do no wrong.

Chapter Eight

The Return to Glory

After the Montréal Canadiens won their franchise's sixth Stanley Cup in 1946, the organization made a change of general managers that would affect the club's future for decades.

Frank Selke cut his management teeth while serving under the tutelage of Conn Smythe in the Toronto Maple Leafs organization. While Smythe was busy serving in the military and Selke had control of the team, several vocal disagreements over player trades led to Smythe getting rid of Selke because he thought Selke was trying to run things without his consent. Smythe fired one of the greatest hockey minds ever, and the Canadiens were more than happy to welcome him into their organization.

In *Lions in Winter*, authors Chrys Goyens and Allan Turowetz explain the impact Selke's firing had on the future of the Canadiens: "With Selke en route to Montréal, Smythe finally could boast that he had an undisputed hand in building an

NHL dynasty. The catch was that the dynasty would turn out to be the Montréal Canadiens, not the Toronto Maple Leafs."

Selke set about a sweeping set of changes to the Montréal farm system that ensured the Canadiens could draw on a never-ending talent pool and saw them establish the greatest teams in National Hockey League history. When Selke arrived, there were only five French-Canadians on the team, far from the Flying Frenchmen of the early days. But Selke extended the Montréal Canadiens' reach into every area of Québec and Canada. By investing in young players coming up in the system, he assured the Canadiens first pick of a fresh supply of young talent.

"We had to do two things: build an organization which on one hand could recruit the very best talent available right across Canada, and at the same time develop the pool of players in our backyard, Québec," Selke recalled in an interview from *Lions in Winter.*

Ironically, while the Canadiens were busy preparing a team for the future, the team Selke helped build in Toronto won the Cup three years in a row, from 1947 to 1949, and again in 1951 against Montréal. But the Canadiens' time was not far behind. From 1946 to 1954, Selke signed players like Doug Harvey, Dollard St-Laurent, Bernard Geoffrion, Dickie Moore, Jacques Plante,

Jean Béliveau and Tommy Johnson, all players who would lead the Canadiens to the greatest years in the franchise's history.

Part of Selke's vision was to make the Montréal organization cultivate a family atmosphere that would ensure the players were willing to give part of themselves to the team and put forth every possible effort to make the Canadiens as a whole the best in the league. Forward Ralph Backstrom described Selke's vision in action, recalling the atmosphere of the team at the time: "We were very close to one another, but I think that winning was the most important thing that we had going for us. When things were not going well, we were frank with one another. Our coaches gave 110 percent, but it was really the players whose pride and deep feelings of commitment sustained the family entity."

Sustaining that family entity was what led Selke to make the biggest change to the Canadiens organization after the tumultuous 1954–55 hockey season.

Chapter Nine

L'Affaire Richard and the Birth of a Dynasty

To truly understand the history of the Canadiens and the lead-up to the Richard Riots of 1955, you have to step out of the sports world and jump into the lives of the people that surrounded the Canadiens during the '40s and '50s.

By the start of the 1954–55 season, the Richard legend had grown to almost religious proportions in the province of Québec. But to the rest of the league, and especially to the National Hockey League's head offices in Toronto, Richard was a spoiled star whose superhero status in Québec gave him carte blanche to do whatever he wanted on the ice. That included several well-publicized run-ins with league president Clarence Campbell over what he considered overly violent behaviour on the part of the Rocket.

Maurice Richard always contended that he was treated differently in the league because he was a Montréal Canadien and, more importantly, a French-Canadian. In a series of articles published in Montréal newspaper *La Presse*, Richard openly criticized Campbell for what he called his hatred of the Canadiens and his racist attitude toward the French people of Québec.

But the Rocket's misdeeds made him a thorn in the side of the NHL. On many occasions, he would give as good as he got. The league's list of violent incidents involving Richard was quite long by the time the 1954 season started.

In 1951, Richard was fined $500 for harassing a referee in the lobby of a hotel after a game. That same year, he got into a fight with a Toronto player and kicked him in the chest with his skate; he also punched out another player during the same scuffle. He was thrown out of the game and fined $50. In 1954, Richard was ordered to pay $1000 for ghost-written articles in a francophone newspaper that openly criticized league president Clarence Campbell as a dictator and a racist; again in 1954, he was fined $250 when he knocked out the two front teeth of Leafs player Bob Bailey and put his glove in the face of the referee who tried to stop him. And those are just some of the more glaring violations.

Richard never cared about the fines levied against him because every time an incident happened, some Québec businessman would send him $1000. Campbell commented, "Richard could do no wrong in Québec. I was always the villain."

The situation escalated to the point where the Rocket was going to be suspended if he was involved in another incident on the ice. General managers and coaches across the league were complaining that Richard was getting away with everything while other players in the league were being fined and suspended for lesser infractions.

On March 13, 1955, Richard was involved in a scuffle that would go down in history as one of the most memorable moments in the Canadiens franchise.

With just a few games remaining in the regular season, it looked like Richard was finally going to win the scoring title after a decade in the National Hockey League. Close behind were teammates Bernie "Boom Boom" Geoffrion and Jean Béliveau, but it was almost certain that the Rocket would retain the title this time.

The Canadiens had played the Bruins two nights before in Montréal in a physical game where Boston players paid specific attention to Richard and pounded him heavily throughout the match. Being the Montréal Canadiens' marquee player, Richard was used to the extra attention on the ice, but near the end of the season, such incidents were starting to get under his skin. On many occasions, it was not uncommon for players to follow up their hard checks with a couple of elbows and a few verbal jabs making fun of his heritage with such witty remarks as "French bastard!" and "Frog!" So for the rematch against the Bruins, Richard was not in the best of moods, and the Boston players wanted to take advantage of this fact.

One player paying particular attention to the Rocket that night was former Canadiens defenceman Hal Laycoe. It was his job to keep Richard from getting free and breaking in on net. The feat was often easier said than done with the Rocket, but Laycoe was up to the task. He was not known as one of the dirtier players in the league, but when a job had to be done, he wasn't known to be the cleanest player, either.

Several times in the first period, Laycoe hacked and slashed at Richard as the Rocket tried to break in on goal. The two men exchanged heated words, and the physical battle continued. Boston fans could sense something was going to happen between the men, and things on the ice were getting very tense.

Then the Rocket came blazing in through the neutral zone and found himself with only one player between him and the net—Hal Laycoe. As Richard tried to make a break for the net, Laycoe realized that he could not stop him with his stick, so he grabbed him around the waist and carried him into the corner with the puck. Determined to stop Richard at any cost, Laycoe proceeded to high-stick Richard on the back of the head. The referee had his arm raised to signal a penalty to Laycoe, but Richard paid no attention.

When he rubbed his head and caught the sight of blood, Richard flew into a rage. With a fierce look in his eyes, he approached Laycoe and swung his stick at him, hitting him on the shoulder and the face. Laycoe dropped his stick and gloves, ready to take him on. Richard had nothing but revenge on his mind and smashed his stick on Laycoe's back. He was about to give him another blow with the stick before linesman Cliff Thompson intervened. But Richard was able to break away from the linesman, retrieve another stick and resume his attack on Laycoe.

Thompson had to employ a more forceful method of restraint, pinning Richard's arm behind his back. Seeing that Richard was tied up with the linesman, Laycoe took the opportunity to punch the defenceless player.

Angered by Thompson's efforts to restrain him, Richard warned the linesman to ease up. "Stop me from the front but not from behind," Richard yelled at Thompson.

Richard broke loose yet again, but the linesman quickly grabbed him from behind once more and kept Richard from getting at Laycoe. Seeing his teammate restrained unfairly, another Montréal player knocked Richard loose from the linesman's grip, allowing Richard to turn around and punch Thompson in the face twice for restraining him from behind.

After the incident, Richard said he felt the punch was justified; he had, after all, given him a warning.

"He wouldn't listen. That's why I hit him," Richard said, looking back on the fight.

When the smoke cleared, Richard was given a match penalty for his numerous violations, and Laycoe was given a 5-minute major for injuring Richard and a 10-minute misconduct for not going to the penalty box when asked.

Richard knew he was going to receive a call from league president Clarence Campbell, but he didn't realize the storm of controversy that would build around his antics on the ice. A hearing was called in Campbell's office to examine both sides of the story, but when all was said and done, Richard was suspended for the remainder of the regular season and the entire playoffs.

Richard's punishment was exceedingly harsh, considering the many infractions by other players in previous years that caused more serious injuries but yielded lesser punishments.

Montréal newspapers were in an uproar over the suspension. French-language papers all had the same hypothesis: If Richard were anglophone, he would not have received such treatment.

The tension could be felt in the city as Montréal moved closer to the end of the regular season. Their hero had been taken out of the playoffs and something needed to be done. French-language newspapers across the city voiced the discontent with the suspension almost on a daily basis. Even the mayor of Montréal chimed in on the affair. "Too harsh a penalty: Mayor Drapeau hoping for a review of sentence," shouted a *La Presse* headline.

Montréal Matin declared: "Victim of yet another injustice, the worst ever, Maurice Richard will play no more this season!"

At the Richard home, phone calls were coming in at all times from fans and supporters promising to do something to avenge the injustice. Campbell also was receiving phone calls at home from Canadiens fans, but of a less supportive nature. Despite receiving numerous threats, Campbell decided to attend the final Canadiens home game on March 17, 1955, against the Detroit Red Wings.

Before the game began, an angry crowd gathered outside the Montréal Forum holding signs in support of Richard and denouncing Campbell as a hater of French Canadians. Inside the Forum, the mood was equally tense before the start of the game. The Red Wings were just two points behind the Canadiens for the regular-season championship. Without Richard in the lineup, if the Canadiens lost the blame would be placed squarely on the shoulders of Campbell.

With the game under way and the attention of the crowd focused on the ice, Campbell tried to make his way quietly to his seat, but was greeted with a loud chorus of boos and the occasional thrown tomato, egg, coin and program. Campbell tried to laugh off the attention, but the crowd's focus was so squarely on him that fans hardly noticed that the Red Wings had taken a 4–1 lead.

Everything began to deteriorate near the end of the first period, when a young man approached Campbell under the pretense of shaking his hand but proceeded to punch him in the face instead. Just as security guards were removing the man from the Forum and restoring relative peace to the building at the end of the period, someone threw a tear-gas grenade a few rows from Campbell. Thick, acrid smoke began to fill the air as the crowd scrambled for the exits.

When the Forum crowd mixed with the thousands of angry fans waiting outside, the situation quickly began to degenerate. What started out as a large group of angry fans turned into an angry mob that began throwing bottles, smashing windows and even setting fire to a newspaper stand. The 250 police officers who were called in had trouble holding back the 10,000 or more people who wanted to vent their rage.

Montréal writer Hugh MacLennan, who was at the game that night, later explained the nature of the riot: "To understand the feelings of the crowd that night is to understand a good bit of the social conditions of Québec of the 1950s."

It was more than just a riot over a hockey player; it was about yet another injustice done to a francophone by Quebec's ruling anglophone class. People found common ground with the Rocket and how he had to work for everything he got. When his hard-earned place on the team was taken away so easily by the aristocratic Campbell, regular people, not only hockey fans, took offence.

After the riots, Richard tried to remain as impartial as he could, but the Rocket could not help voicing his opinion on what started the actual violence: "It was Mr. Campbell who incited the fans. If he had not gone to the game that night…"

Canadiens general manager Frank Selke convinced Richard to go on the radio and address the public in English and French in order to quell any ideas of further violence. After all the fires were put out and Montréalers had a chance to survey the more than $100,000 in damage, the city hung its collective head in shame at what it had done in the name of its hockey hero.

That year, Richard lost the scoring title to teammate Geoffrion and could not help his team in its push for the Cup. Without Richard in the lineup, the Canadiens still made it to the Stanley Cup finals, but lost in a close series against the Detroit Red Wings.

Would the Canadiens have won had Richard been playing? Would it have been six consecutive Stanley Cups instead of five? Regardless, the Canadiens returned with Richard the next season and began the greatest dynasty in hockey history. But the events of that St. Patrick's Day night in 1955 remain clear in the memory of those who lived through it and are embedded in the minds of all Canadiens fans.

Chapter Ten

The Greatest Team in Hockey

The Canadiens' fortunes turned around for the 1955–56 season as longtime coach Dick Irvin left the team for Chicago, and Frank Selke hired a hockey old-timer who would coach the greatest years in the Montréal Canadiens' long history.

Management made a few additions to the team on the ice, including forwards Henri Richard (Maurice's brother) and Claude Provost, and defencemen Bob Turner and Jean-Guy Talbot. But the most important change in the team's makeup occurred behind the bench.

Irvin was often called one of the best coaches in the National Hockey League, having taken the teams he coached into the playoffs in all but three of his 28 years behind the bench. But there was always the note attached that he led his teams (Chicago, Toronto and Montréal) all the way to the Stanley Cup just four times in his career.

The often-cantankerous Irvin had been mellowed by his battle with cancer and wanted a job with a little less pressure. During the off-season, the Canadiens announced that they were looking to replace Irvin.

Selke had a long list of potential candidates to choose from: former Maple Leafs player and coach Joe Primeau, former Canadiens defenceman Roger Leger, recently retired Canadiens forward Billy Reay, and former Canadiens star centreman Hector "Toe" Blake.

Selke wanted to give Primeau the job, but team vice-president Ken Reardon insisted that Blake be considered because his coaching style would be the perfect counterpoint to the years of the fiery Irvin behind the bench. That is not to say that Blake was a saint. On the contrary, when he was upset he could be downright mean, which was one of the reasons Selke did not want to hire him. But with approval from Reardon and a blessing from Maurice Richard, Blake became the 13th coach in Habs history.

Blake did not have a difficult job to do during his first year coaching the Canadiens. Selke had assembled a team loaded with all-star veterans and young talent, making Blake's role rather easy. But no matter the team in front of him, Blake still pushed his players to be their best, even if by the end of 1955–56 regular season they were an astonishing 24 points ahead of the second-place Detroit Red Wings.

In an interview in *Lions in Winter* by Goyens and Turowetz, former Habs goalie Jacques Plante explained some of Blake's methods: "The guy knew how to prime you for a game; he knew what button to push to get the most out of guys because he always wanted to maintain the edge."

Referee Red Storey was witness to Blake's temperamental side when things weren't going well for the Canadiens: "I remember that he would close the dressing room door after a bad game and raise the roof in there. But when that door opened to the media, you never heard a bad word from him about any of his players. That kind of class will keep you in white shirts for a long time," Storey said.

The 1955–56 season was a breakout year for the Montréal Canadiens. Apart from dominating the regular season's points race, their players also dominated the scoring leaders category, with four players in the top 10.

Goals were coming so fast and furious, like Jean Béliveau's hat trick in 44 seconds during one power play, that the following year the league ruled that minor penalties would end after a goal was scored against the offending team. Plante dominated in goal that season, recording seven shutouts and leading the league in goals against average with 1.86.

In the playoffs, the Canadiens coasted through the New York Rangers and the Detroit Red Wings to win the Stanley Cup for the eighth time in franchise history. Jacques Plante bettered his regular-season goals against average to a low 1.80, while Jean Béliveau lit the lamp 12 times in the playoffs and had a record 7 goals in thc final series. The finals were also sweet retribution. The Detriot Red Wings beat the Canadiens in the final game of the 1954–55 season on the infamous night of the Richard Riots to win the regular-season title for the seventh straight year and they later beat the Canadiens in game seven of the Stanley Cup finals, so for the Canadiens, especially Maurice Richard, the 1956 Stanley Cup meant a lot.

Although Detroit took back the regular-season title the next year, things rolled smoothly for the Canadiens on all fronts. Maurice Richard took over as the team's captain from Émile Bouchard after the big veteran defenceman retired. With relatively the same cast of players from their 1956 Stanley Cup victory, the Canadiens dominated every aspect of the game, which allowed them to win the Cup for five consecutive years between 1956 and 1960.

At each position, the Canadiens had one all-star that could be relied on to pick up what little slack there was left behind by other players. On defence, the Canadiens boasted one of the best to ever play the game in Doug Harvey. In the five straight years that the Canadiens won the Cup, Harvey took home the Norris Trophy as top defenceman four times. Harvey wasn't simply good at defence. His mastery of checking, blocking shots, stick handling and passing and his all-around intelligence when it came to his position enabled him to keep players away from his goaltender and take complete control of the game whether he had the puck or not.

Guarding the Montréal net for those best years was the eccentric Jacques Plante. The Montréal Canadiens of the early '50s were a good team, but they didn't become a great team until later, when Plante replaced a stumbling Gerry McNeil in the 1953 playoffs. His performance during that time assured coach Irvin that Plante would be their goaltender for the future. Plante's unpredictable style and habit of wandering out of the goaltender's protective crease changed the way the position was played for years to come.

Through the five consecutive Cups, Plante led the regular season and the playoffs in goals against average, taking home the Vezina Trophy five straight times.

But Plante's most memorable and lasting contribution to the game of hockey was that he was the first netminder to regularly wear a face mask for games.

Plante had contemplated the idea of wearing a face mask during a regular-season game, but coach Blake never liked the idea, saying it just wasn't done and he was worried that the goalie would not be able to see the puck clearly. Plante had been working with a designer on different styles of masks, which he regularly used in practice, and he was looking for a good reason to bring his mask out in a regular-season game. His chance came on November 1, 1959, during a game against the New York Rangers. Rangers forward Andy Bathgate shot a blistering backhand, and Plante was hit right in his unprotected face. While receiving a new batch of stitches, the netminder told Blake he would not play the rest of the game if he wasn't allowed to wear his mask. Without any other option, Blake grudgingly agreed, and the mask eventually became required equipment for all goaltenders.

Another key player in the Canadiens' successful run to five straight Stanley Cups and beyond was *"Le Gros Bill!"* Jean Béliveau. Joining the Montréal Canadiens for the 1953–54 season, Béliveau would play his entire career with the team and win an incredible 10 Stanley Cups.

If Maurice Richard was the soul of the Canadiens, Jean Béliveau would represent their legacy. During his long career with the Canadiens, he played in 1287 games and scored 586 goals. His style on the ice was like no other, and fans of hockey in all parts of the country remember Béliveau as one of the best to ever play the game and say that no one else brought the level of class that Béliveau displayed both on and off the ice.

Add to that the scoring ability of Dickie Moore, Henri Richard, Bernie "Boom Boom" Geoffrion and Maurice Richard and it is easy to see how the Canadiens dominated the game completely.

By the 1960 Stanley Cup finals, the Canadiens were in a class all by themselves. They were again at the top of the league at the end of the regular season and were once more the favourites going into the first round of the playoffs against forward Bobby Hull and the Chicago Blackhawks. Even the explosive offence of the Blackhawks could not match the defensive genius of the Canadiens, and the Habs easily swept the series with Jacques Plante earning shutouts in the last two games.

Montréal continued to its fifth straight Cup that year in the finals against the Toronto Maple Leafs, scoring 3 goals in the first 15 minutes of the first period of the first game. The defence held back the Leafs while Plante finished the playoffs with a miserly 1.35 goals against average.

The Canadiens equalled a record set by the Detroit Red Wings in 1952 by winning eight straight games, sweeping their way to the Cup.

Before a subdued crowd at Maple Leaf Gardens in Toronto, the Canadiens celebrated their fifth Cup while hungry reporters scurried around to get a quote from the players.

Doug Harvey best summarized the Canadiens' win: "When you win eight straight games in the playoffs and you win five Cups in a row, there's not a whole lot to get excited about."

This was the last Cup in the Habs dynasty of the '50s, and it was also the last Cup for the Rocket. After 18 years in the NHL, Maurice Richard had put on a lot of weight and slowed down considerably. The fire in his eyes no longer burned with the same passion that once made him the most feared goal scorer in the NHL, and he decided to end his career that year after winning his eighth Stanley Cup. The game of hockey has never seen another like him since—and never will.

Chapter Eleven

The Greatest Rivalry: Montréal versus Toronto

The Montréal Canadiens have been around long enough and have won enough Stanley Cups to earn some bitter rivals, including the Montréal Maroons and the Boston Bruins, but none can compare in history and passion to that of their rivalry with the Toronto Maple Leafs.

The difficulty with the Montréal–Toronto rivalry is that it's hard to pinpoint exactly when it began or if it even started on the ice at all. As long as there has been a city of Toronto, there has been an ingrained, almost genetic tension between its closest rival, Montréal. Long before the establishment of the National Hockey League, Montréal and Toronto had been competing on the political, economic and social issues of the day. There is also the linguistic tension between English-dominated Toronto and French-dominated Montréal.

Disliking Toronto seems to be a Canadian tradition, but the feud with Montréal goes deeper than a simple aversion to the city. Add the powder kegs that were the Montréal Forum and the Maple Leaf Gardens during the '40s and '50s and you have the makings of the best rivalry in hockey to this day. The rivalry began in the '40s but became the stuff of legend in the '60s.

Prior to the '40s, both Montréal and Toronto could not maintain competitive teams and rarely met one another in the post-season (where true rivalries begin). Montréal had its crosstown rivals the Maroons to deal with during the early years of the NHL and could not devote much hatred to the Leafs until later. It wasn't until the arrival of Maurice Richard and Frank Selke in the 1940s that the inbred feelings between the two cities surfaced on the ice.

As Richard ripped up the scoring sheet in his first few years, the Toronto Maple Leafs often were on the receiving end of his record-breaking moments, which built up a natural dislike of the star forward and his teammates.

During the 1944 playoffs, first-place Montréal met third-place Toronto in a series that all the sportswriters predicted would be a cakewalk for the Canadiens. Toronto surprised the Canadiens in the first game by putting up a tight defence and winning by a score of 3–1. But Montréal had an answer during the next game at the Forum, and his name was Maurice Richard. By the end of the second game, Richard had scored all five of the Canadiens' goals in a 5–1 victory. As the Forum crowd chanted Richard's name, the Leafs had found their target.

The next season, the Rocket put his name in the record books again during a game against his favourite whipping boys when he established a new season-high goal-scoring plateau. On February 23, 1945, Maurice Richard had tied former Canadiens great Joe Malone's record of 44 goals in one season and went up against the Toronto Maple Leafs before raucous Forum fans waiting with bated breath for their hero to set a new mark. With just a few minutes remaining in the period, the Leafs thought they had managed to stop the Rocket from getting his goal, but in the blink of an eye, Richard escaped the player assigned to check him and broke in on goaltender Frank McCool to score his 45th goal of the season. Enemy number one in Toronto: Maurice "the Rocket" Richard!

But the Leafs did not realize until it was too late that the Canadiens had more scoring talent than Richard alone. With everyone's attention focused on Richard, the Habs easily took the next three games, finishing off the series before a capacity crowd in Montréal by a score of 11–0.

All but three of the Canadiens in the lineup that night scored a goal, with the defencemen even chipping in on a few goals, sending the Leafs packing until the next year.

As much as Toronto fans hated Richard for his exploits against their team, Toronto management knew that if Richard could be coaxed over to the Leafs, he would take them far. In a cheap attempt to put pressure on Canadiens management to trade Richard, an article was published in the *Globe and Mail* with an accompanying picture of Maurice Richard dressed in a Maple Leafs uniform. Leafs president Conn Smythe knew how important Richard was to the Canadiens, and wanted to use every trick in the book to try and get him to Toronto, but Selke would not even entertain the idea of trading Québec's hero.

"Even if you would give us the entire Leafs team, and even Maple Leaf Gardens, the answer would still be no!" Selke replied.

Imagine how different both teams' histories would have been had Richard been traded to the Leafs. *Quelle horeure*!

The Leafs would turn things around at the end of the '40s, winning three Stanley Cups in a row with the skilled players Selke had helped acquire while serving under Smythe. But the future looked a lot brighter for the Canadiens.

In just a short time, Selke had turned the Canadiens' fortunes around and set his sights on developing a healthy rivalry with his former team. Even before the first game the Canadiens were to play against the Maple Leafs in 1947, Selke was firing challenges to Smythe in Toronto. In a Canadian Press interview before Montréal's first game against Toronto, Selke fired the opening shot at the Leafs when he accused the Toronto defence of playing like wrestlers, always holding on to their opponents. Selke added that he would sign popular wrestler Yvon Robert to deal with the Leafs. Smythe quickly responded to the article, saying Selke was just trying to distract his team.

Despite the obvious promotional reasons for firing insults back and forth, the public bought into it, and the Canadiens and Leafs played before a sold-out crowd for their first game that season, which happened to end in a 1–1 tie.

The back-and-forth verbal jabs between the two teams continued throughout the 1946–47 season as each game between the Leafs and the Canadiens was played without an empty seat in the house.

The Canadiens' chances of making it far into the series took a serious blow when Elmer Lach was taken out for the rest of the season after the Leafs' Don Metz delivered a vicious check sending Lach to the ice, where the Canadiens player hit his head and fractured his skull. Even though the "Punch Line" of Richard, Blake, and Lach had been broken up, the Canadiens made it to the Stanley Cup finals—but so did the Maple Leafs.

Montréal put a good scare into Leafs fans by winning the first game, but Toronto won the series, shutting down Montréal's top scoring lines in hard-checking, defensive games. Over the next few years the Leafs would come out on top in the rivalry, culminating in the famous 1951 Stanley Cup victory when Bill Barilko scored the overtime winner.

But this would be the last hurrah for the Leafs for a number of years. Selke's hard work securing young talent led the Canadiens to 10 straight Stanley Cup final appearances (from 1951 to 1960) and gave Montréal the upper hand in the battle between the two cities.

The rivalry truly heated up during the '60s, when Montréal and Toronto were the best teams in the league and owned the Stanley Cup from 1962 to 1970.

Apart from the occasional menace from the Chicago Blackhawks and the Detroit Red Wings, the Montréal Canadiens and the Toronto Maple Leafs were the dominant forces the league during the '60s. The Blackhawks had the highest-powered offence but could never seem to get their act together long enough in the playoffs to be a serious threat. After their success in the '50s, the Red Wings could never find the right combination of players to bring any power to the post-season until the 1990s. Without a doubt, the 1960s was the decade of Blue and White versus *bleu, blanc, rouge*.

The beginning of the decade saw another three Cup wins in a row for the Leafs. They eliminated the Canadiens from the playoffs in two physically hard-fought series during which their almost 40-year-old Toronto goaltender, Johnny Bower, was the star player. Goaltending was the key ingredient missing from the Canadiens' formula after they traded Jacques Plante in 1963, and they didn't get back on track until the arrival of veteran goalie Lorne "Gump" Worsley.

The 1965 series brought the return of *"Les Glorieux"* with a solid performance in the regular season and a hard-fought opening round of the playoffs against the enemy Leafs. They split the first four games, but the Canadiens were able to get past Bower's goaltending to win the next two games and eventually took home their 13th Stanley Cup.

The rivalry heated up even more when Toronto and Montréal met again in the first round of the 1966 playoffs. Montréal was the odds-on favourite to win the series after finishing 11 points ahead of the Leafs. The Habs had a fast team known for its offensive talent and injection of youthful players, while Toronto had the complete opposite. Although the team could score goals, Toronto coach Punch Imlach knew that his team of aging veterans would be better served by focusing on a more defensive style of game. Imlach decided to replace one aging veteran goaltender for another in the first game, throwing Terry Sawchuk in to defend against the Canadiens on Forum ice.

From the drop of the puck at the start of first period, it was clear to Canadiens coach Toe Blake that his team was not going to have an easy time with the tenacious Leafs squad, whose veteran players showed their experience and created a 2–1 lead by the first intermission. The Canadiens got an earful from Blake in the dressing room between periods and came out harder, playing physically and taking advantage of turnovers. It wasn't until the final minutes of the game, with the score tied at 3, that Jean Béliveau broke lose and scored the game-winning goal.

Toronto was not happy with the loss, and after two days of being left to think about it, they came out hitting hard in the first period of the second game. The bad blood between the two teams was so intense that the referee gave 22 penalties for a total of 55 minutes before the horn sounded the end of the first period.

Canadiens goaltender Worsley did the rest of the work as the Canadiens blanked the Leafs in game two. The Leafs could not recover from the loss and were taken out in four straight as the Canadiens moved on to the finals. They defeated the Detroit Red Wings for their second straight Cup.

The rivals would meet for the last time in a classic Stanley Cup battle before the league expanded in 1967. Although the Canadiens would meet the Maple Leafs two more times in the playoffs in the '70s, the Stanley Cup final series of 1967 has come to define the intense rivalry and history these two Canadian clubs have between them. This was the last year of the "original six," before the National Hockey League expanded to 12 teams. It also happened to be the year of Canada's centennial, and Montréal was hosting the 1967 Expo (World's Fair). The sense of rivalry was in the air long before the final series of 1967 got under way.

The tension between the two cities and the two teams was that much greater because most of the Montréal Canadiens players were from Québec and a large part of the Toronto roster was from around that city. City versus city, a battle to see which had the better hockey team and which had the better fans. Montréal was riding high on the wave of Expo '67 and would have liked nothing more than to add a Stanley Cup celebration to the festivities, but some Leafs players had different ideas.

"We were the underdogs, so we didn't feel the pressure," said Leafs forward Frank Mahovlich in Damien Cox and Gord Stellick's *'67: The Maple Leafs, their Sensational Victory and the End of an Empire*. "Montréal was just going berserk about Expo, and we wanted to do something to deflate a city that assumed the Stanley Cup was going to be part of Expo."

Thus began the sabre-rattling in the cities' papers and on their radio and television shows. Montréal media were confident that the Canadiens could bring home the Cup for Expo '67 and ruin Torontonians' hopes of bringing Stanley to the city for its Centennial celebrations.

Montréal was the definite favourite in the series, having a youthful core of players and coming off a Stanley Cup win in 1966. Toronto, with its group of aging players, would have to rely on experience, hard work and outstanding goaltending from Bower and Sawchuk to have any hope of defeating the Canadiens. It appeared the series was a *fait accompli* in the first game, with the Canadiens controlling every aspect on their way to a 6–2 victory. Sawchuk took the blame for the loss and ceded his place to the much older Bower (41 by this time!) for game two in Montréal.

This was the turning point in the series. Experienced goaltending won out over youth as Toronto's Bower stole the show, blanking the Canadiens while rookie goaltender Rogatien Vachon was good but not good enough against the Leafs, allowing 3 goals. For game three, Toe Blake made some adjustments during the Canadiens' practice and focused on a way to get around the tough forechecking and pressure on the puck.

When the puck was dropped, it seemed the Canadiens' practice had paid off, but once again Bower did everything but stand on his head to keep his team in the game. Vachon was no slouch either in this game, stopping 62 shots to Bower's 54, but in the end the Leafs won the game before a raucous home crowd on a goal by Bob Pulford in the second overtime.

The Canadiens caught a break for game four when Bower was injured during the pre-game skate and was replaced by Sawchuk, who let his team down by allowing 6 goals. History repeated itself as the Canadiens ran over a tired-looking Leafs squad and Vachon looked like he had returned to form, making some key saves that allowed his team to pull ahead. But that was all the Canadiens could muster against the Leafs. Toronto took the final game by a score of 3–1 to win the 13th Stanley Cup in Maple Leafs history.

The Leafs had ruined the Habs' celebrations and had taken away the possibility of another five Cups in a row, but the Canadiens went on to win the Cup in '68 and '69. The sweetest revenge for the Habs, however, was that they would go on to defeat the Leafs two more times in the playoffs in the '70s and have won 10 Stanley Cups since then, while the Leafs, after winning it in '67, are still waiting for their next one.

Chapter Twelve

Into the '70s and Still Going Strong

In 1964, when Frank Selke retired as general manager, he placed the fate of the team in the capable hands of his successor, Sam Pollock. Cutting his teeth under the watchful eye of Selke as he handled the Canadiens' amateur teams, Pollock proved to have a keen eye for talent. Born in the Montréal community of Notre-Dame-de-Grâce, Pollock was perfectly suited to take over from Selke, who had brought so many changes, and more importantly, so much success, during his reign.

The Canadiens Selke left to Pollock were far from being a problem during his first year with the club. Pollock had the talent of veteran players such as Jean Béliveau, Henri Richard and Ralph Backstrom, but he saw the need for change if the team was to continue to be successful into the next decade.

Pollock's vision for the Canadiens was simple but effective: "People have asked me many times how someone goes about building the kind of tradition the Canadiens have enjoyed for so long," Pollock said in an interview in *Lions in Winter*. "It is really quite simple. You build a top-notch organization manned by the best people at all levels. You get each man doing his job on the ice and off the ice and all of a sudden, you're a winner."

That was easy for Pollock to say, considering he inherited a winning organization from Selke. But the hardest part was keeping that winning tradition going, and none was better at it than Sam Pollock, especially as the National Hockey League underwent its most significant changes with the expansion and the arrival of the World Hockey Association.

Some of Pollock's earliest changes to the team saw the departure of Jean-Guy Talbot, Charlie Hodge, and Dave Balon in favour of youthful players like Rogatien Vachon, Pete Mahovlich, Serge Savard, Guy Lapointe and Jacques Lemaire. Pollock's faith in the young players paid off in his first years with the team as the Canadiens took the Cup in '68 and '69 and teams such as Boston and Chicago waited in the wings for the Canadiens to falter. Not even the departure of Blake in 1968, long considered the best coach in the National Hockey League, could slow the Habs down.

From 1955 to 1968, Hector "Toe" Blake had served as coach during one of the most successful periods in the Canadiens' history. Under his tutelage, players such as Henri Richard, Ralph Backstrom, Yvan Cournoyer, Claude Provost and many more would become some of the best in the league. But during his last years coaching Montréal, the quiet (when he wanted to be) Blake was becoming more temperamental with the media, and in one case, he even went after a spectator in Los Angeles. With a heavy heart, the "Old Lamplighter," as he was known in his playing days, retired from his job behind the bench, entrusting the coaching position to 30-year-old Claude Ruel.

But after two seasons, the pressures of the job started to eat away at the young coach, and at the end of a game against the Minnesota North Stars in November 1970, Ruel decided to leave the team and cede his place to Al MacNeil.

But MacNeil was not a popular selection with the Canadiens' influential veterans, and with an anglophone coach taking over the team just after the October Crisis of 1970 (when an extremist nationalist group in Québec known as the FLQ kidnapped and killed a public official) the situation in the dressing room began to fall apart.

"The team was pretty established and they balked at some of the things I wanted to do," MacNeil said.

No player was more vocal in his contempt of MacNeil than Henri Richard. Things between coach and player had become so bad that during a game against the Los Angeles Kings in the 1970–71 season, Richard slapped MacNeil during an argument about his playing time. Newspapers seized on the opportunity to publicize this latest rift between the proud bearer of the Richard name (worth its weight in gold in Québec) and his anglo coach, adding more fuel to the fire of a turbulent year in Montréal.

Despite the tension between the coach and the veterans, the Canadiens managed to finish out the season in fourth place overall. MacNeil had hoped the disagreements would cease during the playoffs, but things only got worse. Montréal made it over its largest postseason hurdle in a hard-fought seven-game series in the first round. Goalie Ken Dryden was the star of the series, stopping the powerful Bruins offence of Bobby Orr, Phil Esposito and John Bucyk.

During the series against the Minnesota North Stars in the semifinals, the tension in the Canadiens dressing room made it into the local press. In game four, Minnesota needed a win to tie the series or face elimination. The team was playing hard and had taken the lead by the end of the second period. The Canadiens needed a spark, and their usual go-to-guy, John Ferguson, was benched the entire third period and watched in frustration as his team lost by a score of 5–2. After the game, Ferguson blew up at MacNeil and refused to play the rest of the series. Toe Blake had to be called out of retirement to defuse the situation in the dressing room and get Ferguson back on the team. Despite the sage advice from Blake, tension continued to escalate after the Canadiens disposed of the North Stars and headed into the finals against the Chicago Blackhawks.

With the series tied at two apiece, things got out of hand between the players and MacNeil after a 2–0 loss in game five. After riding the pine for the majority of the game, Henri Richard could no longer hold back his contempt for MacNeil and publicly called him incompetent and the worst coach that he had ever played for in his entire career. Once the papers printed the story in bold letters on their front pages, MacNeil started receiving death threats. A security guard had to be placed near the coach during the next game at the Forum, and even at MacNeil's home to protect his wife and young daughter. MacNeil looked back on the incident in an interview in *Lions In Winter.*

"I was playing the kids a lot and after game five, Henri, who had been sitting on the bench a lot, blasted me. He said I was a bad coach. Then the Forum started getting phone calls with bomb threats. Remember this was after the Kidnap Crisis and the War Measures Act and French–English relations were not so good."

After a brief summer holiday, Al MacNeil returned to Montréal and advised Pollock that he would no longer coach the Canadiens with this kind of stress on him and his family.

After a couple of years of trying to get the Canadiens' goaltending situation straightened out, Pollock's acquisition of the young rookie sensation Ken Dryden finally solved their goaltending dilemma. It proved to be one of the most important decisions for the Habs' future that decade. After helping them to the Cup as a rookie during that turbulent 1970–71 season, the goaltender who wanted to be a lawyer won the Conn Smythe Trophy as the most valuable player in the playoffs. Not a bad accomplishment considering the performance of the Canadiens' Frank Mahovlich, who scored 14 goals and 13 assists to lead the playoffs in scoring.

Often, the success of the Canadiens rose and fell with the performance of their goaltender, and now they had one of the best in the game.

The 1971 preseason was a very important one for the Canadiens organization. Working feverishly to bring his team back together, Pollock made two important moves that changed the future of the team for the rest of the decade.

Following an angry and vocal disagreement with the St. Louis Blues management, Scotty Bowman was fired from his position as coach after three seasons. Since the Canadiens were in need of a coach, Bowman was the first person Pollock called after MacNeil left the organization. If Bowman could lead a team of aging, mediocre Blues players to three consecutive Stanley Cup finals, then imagine what he could to with the Montréal Canadiens.

Pollock's next move would help the Canadiens on the ice. All the scouts said the same thing about Guy Lafleur. The 19-year-old player was a creative skater and a natural goal-scorer. He was sure to be in demand during the 1971 NHL draft. The problem for Pollock was that the Canadiens were to pick later in the draft because they had finished high in the standings the year before. Surely, they were going to lose out on Lafleur by the time their turn came around.

But Pollock was no fool; he knew the Canadiens would need a top pick, and the year before he had traded the Canadiens' top pick of 1970 with the California Golden Seals' top pick of

1971, which meant that Lafleur was now up for grabs. The Canadiens wasted no time signing the young French-Canadian star that everyone had hoped would be a replacement for the retired Jean Béliveau.

"Le Démon Blond," as he would be nicknamed by Montréal fans, had a decent start with the Canadiens in 1971, scoring 29 goals and 35 assists in his first season, but it wasn't until three years later that the demon was fully unleashed. By 1975, Guy Lafleur found his place on the team, he knew his role and relished the attention Montréal fans and media accorded him, and he became the new poster boy for Québec hockey.

With some of the pieces in place, the Canadiens won another Stanley Cup in 1973, defeating the Chicago Blackhawks again to take home their 18th Cup in franchise history. Montréal lost in the early rounds of the 1974 and 1975 playoffs, but the two years of experience helped the younger players on the team develop and allowed Bowman to fully implement his strategy to create the most successful team in hockey history.

The 1976 Stanley Cup-winning roster of the Montréal Canadiens was one every coach dreams about. It included Doug Risebrough, Guy Lafleur, Yvan Cournoyer, Réjean Houle, Pete Mahovlich, Steve Shutt, Jacques Lemaire and Bob Gainey, just to name a few up front. The Habs also had the big three defencemen Larry Robinson, Guy Lapointe and Serge Savard, with Ken Dryden and backup goalie Michel Larocque rounding out the team.

The Canadiens' dominance of the last half of the 1970s began even before the start of the 1975 regular season. The Philadelphia Flyers were coming off their second straight Stanley Cup victory and wanted to establish their physical presence early to let other top teams know they wanted the Cup a third time. In a preseason match against the Philadelphia Flyers, the Canadiens weren't about to let them establish anything. Montréal was dominating the game 6–2 when Bobby Clarke decided to take a run at Hab Doug Risebrough. The Flyers were surprised by the sudden attack from the Canadiens, and they were beaten up badly before their own fans.

Montréal winger Steve Shutt knew that something special occurred that night: "We won the Stanley Cup that night. It just wasn't official until next May."

The Canadiens finished their regular season with an incredible 58 wins and only 11 losses for a total of 127 points. They were the favourites going into the playoffs, with the Flyers right behind in the regular-season standings with 118 points. Montréal disposed of the Chicago Blackhawks in the quarterfinals and the New York Islanders were still a few years away from providing a decent challenge, falling aside in five games in the semifinals to the more powerful Canadiens.

This set up a rematch of the preseason game between the Canadiens and the Flyers in the Stanley Cup finals. The Flyers won their two Cups using a rough, hard-hitting style that had earned them the nickname the "Broad Street Bullies," but intimidation no longer worked on the Canadiens, who had exorcised those demons in the preseason game's brawl. Executing Scotty Bowman's plans perfectly, the Canadiens managed to keep the tough guys at bay and sweep the series for their 19th Stanley Cup.

Hard to believe things could get any better, but they did.

Yvan Cournoyer remembered the feeling after beating the Flyers that year: "When we won against Philly, we had to create an example. You don't have to be big and rough, and fight all the time, to win the Stanley Cup. We had the size and we had the scorers. If you don't score, you don't win, no matter how good a fighter you are."

While one-dimensional teams like the Flyers did well during the regular season, their toughness could not sustain them through the playoffs. Montréal had both a good offence and a good defence that made them the best team in the league from 1975 to 1979. For the 1976–77 season, the Canadiens were the undisputed champions of the league. They only lost one home game all year, and finished the season with a record of 60–8–12 for a total of 132 points.

For the team having the most successful season in hockey history, the hardest part of a coach's job is to keep the players' minds focused on winning. Complacency was Scotty Bowman's biggest threat, and he avoided it the only way he knew how. Steve Shutt characterized Bowman's coaching method in Dick Irvin's book *The Habs*: "He realized that the only team that could beat our team was ourselves. We had such a good team that petty little grievances could develop that might bring the team down. So what Scotty did, he made himself the focal point. The one thing we had in common was that everybody hated Scotty."

Some would say it's easy to coach a team loaded with talent like the Canadiens were in the late '70s, but ego and pride have a way of creeping in, and Bowman was a master at keeping the players focused. Often, he would call out players who were not playing their best in the media and publicly embarrass them in an attempt to get them to elevate their game. Bowman was not a pleasant man to be around when the Canadiens were losing, and it was this drive to win that kept the players focused on the task at hand.

They might not have liked Bowman, but they trusted everything he wanted to do with the legendary team.

Guy Lafleur finished the season as the top scorer with 136 points, and linemate Steve Shutt finished with 60 goals and a total of 105 points, the best numbers of his career. The Canadiens were the definite favourites going into the playoffs.

Their first opponents, the St. Louis Blues, provided little challenge as the Canadiens swept the series and moved into the semifinals against the up-and-coming New York Islanders. The young team still wasn't ready for playoff success, and the Canadiens moved on to the finals once again after six games. Although the Bruins were the top team of the Adams Division, in the finals they were no match for the Habs, who had never lost to the Bruins in a playoff series since 1943. Boston would have to wait another year to get a shot at beating the Canadiens (and would have to wait until 1988 before they finally beat the Habs in a playoff series), because they were swept in four straight for the Canadiens' 20th Stanley Cup.

When the silverware was handed out at the end of the season, the Canadiens took home a remarkable nine trophies: the Stanley Cup, Prince of Wales Trophy, Art Ross Trophy (awarded to Guy Lafleur), Hart Trophy (awarded to Guy Lafleur), Norris Trophy (awarded to Larry Robinson), Vezina Trophy (awarded to Michel Larocque and Ken Dryden), Adams Trophy (awarded to Scotty Bowman), Leaster Pearson Trophy (awarded to Guy Lafleur) and finally, the Conn Smythe Trophy (awarded to Guy Lafleur).

The Canadiens remained at the top for the next two seasons, only falling behind in the regular season to the New York Islanders in 1978–79 by one point. But it was again in the playoffs that the Canadiens knew how to shine, easily defeating the Toronto Maple Leafs in the quarterfinals. It was only in the semifinals that the Canadiens hit a bump on their way to their 22nd Stanley Cup.

The Canadiens were favoured to win their series against Boston, but head Bruins coach Don Cherry had other plans. After fighting off elimination in game six, the Bruins went into game seven confident that they could knock off the defending Cup champions with a little hard work and a little luck. Late in game seven, it looked like the Bruins were actually going to pull off the upset of the season, leading the game by a score of 4–3 with just a few minutes left on the clock. The Montréal Forum was eerily quiet as the fans hoped their team could come up with the miracle goal. With precious seconds ticking away, the Canadiens got the break they so desperately needed.

Out of the corner of his eye, the referee noticed Don Cherry waving his arms erratically in a vain attempt to call a player back to the bench. But it was too late: the referee had seen that the Bruins had too many men on the ice, and he immediately whistled the play dead and assessed the Boston bench a two-minute minor. Suddenly, the Forum was filled with noise as the fans got to their feat to cheer on their Habs in the final moments of the game with a berth in the Stanley Cup finals on the line.

Then, it happened. With just under two minutes remaining in the third period, Jacques Lemaire broke through the neutral zone, crossed over the Bruins blue line and fed a drop pass to Guy Lafleur, who was streaking down the right side. Without hesitating, Lafleur blasted the puck at a sharp angle that found the corner of the net past surprised Bruins goaltender Gilles Gilbert. The Canadiens had earned themselves some overtime.

Don Cherry would later write about the incident in his autobiography: "I felt disgusted with myself for letting it happen. Sometimes when you have too many men on the ice, it's the players' fault. But not this time. I hadn't spelled out the assignments plainly enough."

The Canadiens, feeling the momentum shift in the building, came out the stronger team in sudden death. The Bruins, still dazed from the Lafleur goal, looked tired and crestfallen. The skilled Canadiens immediately jumped on the opportunity. Mario Tremblay crossed into the Bruins zone and shot a pass over to Yvon Lambert, who tipped the puck off Gilbert's pad and into the net for the winning goal. The Forum exploded as the Canadiens cleared their bench and swarmed Lambert. The team advanced to the finals against the New York Rangers, where they won in five games and lifted the Cup for the 22nd time in their history.

Chapter Thirteen

The Coming of St. Patrick

After their fourth consecutive Stanley Cup victory in 1979, things began to unravel in the Canadiens organization. Scotty Bowman was the first and most important departure for the team. After having been passed over as the replacement for Sam Pollock in the position of general manager in favour of the inexperienced Irving Grundman, Bowman decided to pursue his career with the Buffalo Sabres as general manager and coach.

To the shock of many, one of Grundman's first decisions was to hire Bernie Geoffrion as coach of the Canadiens. Geoffrion had coached twice before with the New York Rangers and the Atlanta Flames, but he had left both jobs because of the pressure and for health reasons. It didn't make much sense to anyone at the time that Geoffrion was hired for a coaching job in the most pressure-filled city in hockey. Geoffrion did not last long before the strain of coaching the

Canadiens got to him, and he was forced to leave his position only 30 games into the season because of stress. Geoffrion was replaced mid-season by the familiar face of Claude Ruel, whom Grundman called upon in his desperation for a replacement coach.

On the ice, the Canadiens lost some of the key ingredients to their most recent success. After only eight seasons in the National Hockey League, all-star goaltender Ken Dryden decided to leave the sport completely in favour of pursuing a career in law. After six Stanley Cups and countless awards, Dryden no longer felt that the roar of the crowd and the thrill of victory were enough, and he moved on. Joining him in the exodus was Jacques Lemaire, who surprised everyone by leaving the National Hockey League to joining a club in Switzerland as a player and coach. The final blow to the Canadiens dynasty came when Yvan Cournoyer announced that he would no longer make his patented speedy moves up the ice because his chronic back problems were forcing him to leave the game he loved. The Canadiens still had a good team, but they had lost a group of players they could rely on to get them past difficult points in a season. At the end of the 1980 regular season, the Canadiens finished third overall in the league, and although they were not the favourites, they seemed ready to make a decent run toward the finals. Ruel had done a respectable job all season, but he was relying heavily on his veteran players. By the time the Canadiens met the Minnesota North Stars in the quarterfinals, most of Montréal's top players were either injured or out completely. The Canadiens lost the series in seven games and ended their chances of matching their team record of five consecutive Stanley Cups.

The Canadiens had two good seasons between 1980 and 1982, but they bowed out early in the playoffs to the young, high-scoring Edmonton Oilers in 1981 and to their provincial rivals, the Québec Nordiques, in 1982. Things just kept getting worse for the Canadiens as the veterans they had come to rely on started to show their age and the young players they had been calling up from the minors just weren't picking up the slack. By the end of the 1984 season, the Canadiens managed only 75 points. They did make it all the way to the Eastern Conference finals, but the much stronger, three-time Stanley Cup–champion New York Islanders defeated the Canadiens in six games.

So it was rebuilding time for the Montréal Canadiens. The media and the fans were calling for a change in the organization after several years of management issues and poor draft choices. The Canadiens' most notable draft blunder came in 1980, when they had the first overall pick and selected Doug Wickenheiser instead of Denis Savard, who went to the Chicago Blackhawks. While Savard went on to have an excellent career with the Hawks, scoring a career high 131 points in 1988, Wickenheiser only managed a career high of 55 points in his final full season with the Canadiens in 1984.

The Canadiens also tried a few new coaches to get themselves out of their losing ways, even employing former Hab Jacques Lemaire. But nothing seemed to be working. Over the summer of 1985, the Canadiens made several changes and add a few new faces that would bring some pride back to the name *"Les Glorieux!"*

Guy Lafleur hung up his skates during the 1984–85 season because he could no longer spoil the Montréal fans like he was used to doing. After 14 seasons with the Canadiens, Lafleur had lost some of the flair for goal scoring that earned him such a loyal following in Montréal. During his last game at the Forum, however, the 18,000 spectators stood on their feet and chanted: "Guy! Guy! Guy!" one last time for Lafleur in a Canadiens uniform. Jacques Lemaire was fired as coach after two less-than-perfect seasons and was replaced by his assistant, Jean Perron. Former Canadiens captain Serge Savard, now the team's general manager, decided with the departure of

Lafleur to go with a distinctly youthful feel to the team.

For the start of the 1985–86 season, the Montréal Canadiens had eight rookies in the lineup: Stéphane Richer, Patrick Roy, Kjell Dahlin, Sergio Memesso, Brian Skrudland, Mike Lalor, Shayne Corson and Steve Rooney. They would add to the list of rookies by the end of the season with Claude Lemieux and John Kordic. The season was a mediocre one for the Canadiens, who finished with 87 points, second in their division, and unlikely to make it far in the playoffs given the stronger teams ahead like the Philadelphia Flyers, Washington Capitals, Edmonton Oilers, and Québec Nordiques. At this time, Montréal wasn't known for its offensive talent, with only one player, Mats Naslund, making it into the top 10 in scoring with 110 points. However, the team had a tenacious group of rookies, led by one of the greatest defensive captains in the game, Bob Gainey. But the most important ingredient for the Canadiens entering the 1986 Stanley Cup playoffs was a skinny rookie goaltender named Patrick Roy.

Drafting him 51st overall, the Canadiens took a big risk on the relative unknown from Québec City. In his final year in the Québec Major Junior Hockey League with the Granby Bisons, Patrick Roy recorded a 5.55 goals against average.

These were not the numbers of a future Hall of Fame goaltender, but Canadiens scouts told general manager Serge Savard that Roy was worth the risk.

Roy made his debut with the team during the 1985–86 regular season and impressed the coach and general manager enough to earn a spot with the Habs. He played in 47 regular-season games and earned a 3.35 goals against average. Not impressive numbers, but the young goalie was confident that he could take the team far into the playoffs.

Roy proved himself worthy in the first round of the playoffs against the Boston Bruins, backstopping the Canadiens through three close games to sweep the series. Skeptical Montréal fans who had reserved their praises for the rookie during the season started to come around as the young goaltender made the difference in many playoff games.

He was outstanding again during the Hartford Whalers series that went into overtime in game seven, and he shut down the New York Rangers in the conference finals to take the Canadiens into the finals for the first time since their last Cup win in 1979.

The Calgary Flames had just come out of two gruelling series that they won by the skin of their teeth against the Edmonton Oilers and the

St. Louis Blues, and they could not keep up with the young legs of the Canadiens. Patrick Roy shut the door for the remainder of the series after giving up 5 goals in the first game, leading the Canadiens to their 23rd Stanley Cup. Roy's amazing 1.92 goals against average and clutch performances earned him his first Conn Smythe award.

After he had played only one full season with the Canadiens, Montréal fans had already started chanting his name, "Roouu-ahh, Roouu-ahhh," and the first few signs with St. Patrick written on them began popping up around the Forum. A French-Canadian goaltender in Montréal was an instant hero, but Roy also made games fun for fans to watch because of his peculiar habits.

It has always been known that goaltenders are a strange lot. It is against human nature to willingly put yourself in front of a frozen rubber puck speeding toward you at over 100 kilometres per hour. The goaltender is often a solitary type that thrives on the pressures of the game. As they don't have a direct part in the team dynamic on the ice like the forwards or defencemen do, often the goaltenders' worst enemies are themselves.

To combat this self-defeating aspect of his position, Patrick Roy developed a strong competitive attitude that enabled him to deal with the pressures of his role and of playing for the Montréal Canadiens, whose history of goaltending excellence goes all the way back to Georges Vézina. Roy had a strange set of habits that he always contended kept him focused on the game, habits his teammates and his fans were more than willing to put up with as long as he kept winning.

One of the most obvious eccentricities that stayed with him throughout his career was the way he constantly moved his head as if he were trying to scratch his face with his shoulder. Another Roy classic was his habit of talking to his goalposts before an important face-off in his zone. If he didn't make a save, his goalposts often got him out of a jam, so he needed to make sure they were ready.

Aside from the peculiar behaviour, Roy was first and foremost one of the best students of the game. His ability to predict the movements on the ice and whether a player would make a pass or try to make a shot is one of main reasons for his success. His athleticism is up there with the greatest of goaltenders, but what set him apart was his mental focus on the game. That was why he flourished as a young goaltender in the pressure-filled arena that is the Montréal Forum. Having such a heavy weight on his shoulders early in his career made it easier for

Roy to succeed under pressure and focus on winning games. The early success and confidence in his game led to a certain bravado in his character that became legendary over his years with the Montréal Canadiens and later with the Colorado Avalanche.

This confidence was necessary in Montréal, where the team seems to live and die by the success of its goaltenders. After their Cup-winning season, the Canadiens rode Roy's early success to a decent place in league standings, but they were playing during a time when Wayne Gretzky and the Edmonton Oilers were dominating the league with their high-powered offence, and the Canadiens had little chance in the playoffs with such a young team. But by the 1988–89 season, Patrick Roy was the king of the Habs.

St. Patrick, as many were now calling him, was having an excellent season in front of the Canadiens net. He even broke a record set 45 years previously by Bill Durnan by winning 26 consecutive home games. He would add another amazing run at the end of the season, winning 29 games straight and securing the William Jennings Trophy (for fewest goals against) for the third year in a row with his goaltending partner, Brian Hayward.

The Canadiens were relying on his goaltending as they went into the 1989 playoffs as one of the top teams. Now under the control of Pat Burns, a former police officer turned hockey coach, the Canadiens finished the season at the top of their division and faced off against the lowly Hartford Whalers in the first round.

The Canadiens easily made their way through the Whalers in four straight games and once again beat up on the poor Bruins, who had finally defeated the Canadiens in the playoffs the year before but went right back to their losing ways in the division finals, taken out by the Habs in five games. Patrick Roy was once again the number one player on the team. The Canadiens did not really have a reliable goal-scoring star in their lineup the likes of a Lafleur or a Richard, so it came down to tight defence and solid goaltending to get the Canadiens through to the final after disposing of the Philadelphia Flyers in six games.

The Stanley Cup finals were a repeat of the 1986 finals with Calgary, and the Flames were hoping to reverse their fortunes this time against Patrick Roy and the Canadiens. The series was close, with no team winning a game by more than 2 goals. They were two evenly matched teams that practised a defensive style of hockey, making for a series that could go either way. But history did not repeat itself as the Flames received stellar performances from goaltender

Mike Vernon and their all-star defenceman, Al MacInnis. Calgary won the series in six games and sent rookie coach Pat Burns, who had been hoping to equal Jean Perron's rookie success, home without a Cup. The Canadiens didn't finish the season empty-handed, however, as Burns took home the Jack Adams Trophy as best coach, Roy took home another Vézina Trophy and Chris Chelios won the James Norris Trophy as the league's best defenceman.

During the 1980s, when the Habs were trying to rekindle some of their team's past glory, they lost some of the people that helped build the legend of the Montréal Canadiens.

Frank Selke, general manager of the Canadiens from 1946 to 1964, who saw the Canadiens through some of their most successful and most cherished years and attended Canadiens home games until the end of his life, passed away at the age of 92 on July 3, 1985.

On February 26, 1986, the Canadiens and hockey lost goaltending legend Jacques Plante, who died at the age of 57 after a lengthy battle with stomach cancer. He had won six Stanley Cups with the Canadiens and countless other awards. Goaltenders to this day cite Plante among some of their biggest influences for the way he approached the game and for his ability to never be controlled by it as well.

A few years later, the Canadiens lost another big part of their 1950s dynasty when defensive mastermind Doug Harvey passed away in 1989 on the day after Christmas. Harvey had been battling alcoholism for years and at one point ended up homeless, sleeping in abandoned railway cars. When the Montréal Canadiens organization learned of his situation, they offered him a job with the team's scouting division, but his many years of alcohol abuse had done their damage, and Harvey finally succumbed to cirrhosis of the liver.

But new players took up the torch and looked to the future to bring the Canadiens back to glory. The rookie team that had won the Cup in 1986 was now looking a little older, and although it continued to perform well in the regular and post-seasons, the Canadiens would have to make a few changes to the lineup before the team would achieve success again.

Chapter Fourteen

The Twenty-Fourth Cup

After three raucous years behind the bench as the Canadiens coach, Pat Burns could no longer take the criticisms from the press and the pressure that goes with being the bench boss of the most successful franchise in hockey history. During the summer of 1992, Burns accepted an offer from Toronto to coach the Maple Leafs. His replacement would be Jacques Demers, a good coach who had never taken a team to the finals but had some success in reviving the pitiful Detroit Red Wings in the late '80s.

Demers inherited a young team with a core of veteran players who would lead the Canadiens to one of their best seasons since their last run to the Cup in 1989. Veteran players such as Guy Carbonneau, Denis Savard (who joined the team in 1990), Patrick Roy and Brian Bellows helped young players such as John Leclair, Stephane Lebeau and Gilbert Dionne position the Canadiens in third place in their division. There were some questions about the performance of Patrick Roy during the regular season. He posted a 3.20 goals against average, his highest since his rookie year, but as Roy had proven many times before, he was at his best when the pressure was at its greatest.

Even with this quality lineup, no one expected the Canadiens to go far against other teams such as the defending Stanley Cup champion Pittsburgh Penguins, or the Boston Bruins, Chicago Blackhawks and Detroit Red Wings. The Canadiens had an outside chance, but two games into their first playoff series against the Québec Nordiques, it looked like the sports pundits had guessed right on the Canadiens' hopes for 1993.

Despite the 2–0 series deficit, Demers was not worried about his team, and he was especially confident in the performance of his number one goaltender, Patrick Roy. The Montréal press had been all over Roy for his less-than-inspiring performances in games one and two after Roy gave up 7 goals in total. Demers knew his goaltender could turn the team's fortunes around when push came to shove and laughed off suggestions that he put backup goaltender André Racicot in nets for the next game in Montréal.

In the Canadiens dressing room before the start of game three, Roy assured his teammates that if they took the lead, he would not let in more than one goal. The Canadiens won the game in overtime by a score of 2–1. Canadiens rookies stepped up and delivered the necessary goals during the rest of the series while Roy was outstanding in shutting down the Nordiques' impressive scoring line. The Canadiens won the next three games to move on to the next round against the Buffalo Sabres.

With their typical flair for the dramatic, the Canadiens won their first game by a score of 4–3 and then won the next three games by the same score, and all the games were won in overtime. That was five overtime wins in a row for the Canadiens, who would continue their winning streak into the next round against the New York Islanders.

With the majority of the top contenders taken out in the first round, the Canadiens' prospects for making it to the finals were higher now that they were riding the success of two hard-fought series. Few of the players were injured or tired, and Roy was having an excellent run that reminded many of his rookie playoff push to the Cup. The New York Islanders had just come off a hard-fought seven-game series against the Pittsburgh Penguins and looked tired facing the fresh legs of the Canadiens. The Canadiens added two more overtime wins in a five-game series victory over the Islanders to move on to the Stanley Cup finals for the first time since they lost to the Calgary Flames in 1989.

The Canadiens had several days' rest before they found out they would play Los Angeles after the Kings won a long, hard series against the Toronto Maple Leafs. There had been hopes all across Canada for a rematch of the 1967 Leafs versus Canadiens finals, but fate—or a player named Gretzky—had different plans. The Kings made it to the finals for the first time in their history since joining the league in 1967. This year would be Montréal's 34th appearance in the finals.

Wayne Gretzky hadn't been to the Stanley Cup finals since his blockbuster trade to the Kings from the Edmonton Oilers in 1988, and he wanted desperately to prove he could win a Cup with another team. For game one in Montréal, it looked like Gretzky was going to take over the series as he led his team to a 4–1 victory on the strength of his goal and 3 assists. But game two in Montréal would prove the turning point in the series and one of the most memorable events in hockey history.

Game two was a fast-paced, action-filled affair that drove everyone gathered at the Forum crazy with all the close chances on net for both teams. Patrick Roy was outstanding, keeping his young team in the game with some miraculous saves, but the Kings managed to sneak 2 goals by him, leaving the Canadiens down by one goal with only a few minutes remaining in the game.

Jacques Demers did not want his team to be down two games to none in the series like they were against Québec earlier in the playoffs. With just over two minutes remaining on the clock in the third period and his team down 2–1, Demers made a controversial call that changed the course of the series.

Demers had noticed earlier that there was something fishy about the curve in Kings defenceman Marty McSorley's stick, but he had not said anything, preferring to hold on to the information in case of an emergency. With his team down by one goal and the momentum of the series on the line, Demers called over referee Kerry Fraser and asked him to verify McSorley's stick for an illegal curve. Fraser took the offending stick from McSorley and went to measure the blade at the penalty-box area. Demers paced back and forth while the referee deliberated with the other officials. Demers' hunch was right: the stick did have an illegal curve, and McSorley was given a two-minute minor.

With nothing to lose, Demers took Patrick Roy out of the net in favour of an extra attacker for a 6-on-4 power play. Montréal defenceman Éric Desjardins scored the equalizer from a point shot past Kings netminder Kelly Hrudey. At only 51 seconds into overtime, Desjardins scored his third goal of the game, giving the Canadiens the crucial win and the momentum in the series, which was going back to Los Angeles. After the game, Kings coach Barry Melrose was visibly upset about the sudden turn of events near the end of the game.

"I don't believe in winning that way!" said Melrose, trying to invoke unwritten rules of hockey conduct, but rules are rules and Jacques Demers used them to his advantage to give his team the much-needed chance at victory.

"Without being cocky, when it comes to overtime, we just feel we can win," Demers said after the game two overtime victory. It was the Canadiens' eighth-straight overtime win.

Confidence in the Canadiens dressing room was at an all-time high. After their upset win in game two, the Canadiens managed to shut down Gretzky and the Kings offence and eked out another overtime win in game three. Patrick Roy was again the story of the series, stealing games from the Kings often with a single save. Game four went into yet another overtime period, but Roy was not worried about the outcome for one single second. He was so confident in overtime that after he robbed forward Tomas Sandstrom on a breakaway, television cameras caught Roy taunting Sandstrom by winking at him to show just how relaxed he was in goal.

The Canadiens rode the wave of confidence through the fifth game and defeated the Kings by a score of 4–2 to win their 24th Stanley Cup. Once again, a group of young, underrated players rose to the occasion when the team needed it most, and their veteran goaltender was there each time to bail the players out when necessary. For his troubles, Patrick Roy won the Conn Smythe Trophy as the playoff's most valuable player for the second time in his career.

Montréal was in full celebration mode. You could see and feel the joy running through everyone after the Canadiens won the Cup, but the celebrations turned ugly when a few drunken revellers took off on a rampage through the streets, breaking windows, setting fires, standing on top of buses and looting anything they could get their hands on. Montréal police were overwhelmed by the sheer number of people who had come out to celebrate the Canadiens' victory and could do little to stem the destruction. When the celebrations died down, Montréal was left with a hefty $1-million bill for damages and a huge sense of shame at having turned the Canadiens victory into a display of bad behaviour.

With a similar lineup to their previous Stanley Cup-winning season, the Canadiens started the 1993–94 season with promise and had a decent year, but they could not bring back the same level of success in the playoffs and were eliminated by the Boston Bruins in the first round. Jacques Demers got a lot of flack in the press for allowing the defending Stanley Cup champs to be defeated so early in the playoffs. He also began hearing complaints from management about the Canadiens' performance.

After the disastrous 1994–95 season, when for the first time in 25 years the Canadiens failed to make the playoffs, Jacques Demers' tenure as coach was on thin ice. When the Canadiens started the 1995–96 regular season without making a major dent in their win column, Canadiens team president Ronald Corey decided to clean house.

It would be a decision that would affect the Canadiens for years, some say even to this day—one that plunged the Canadiens into some of the worst years in the history of the franchise.

Chapter Fifteen

A Franchise in Trouble and a Glimmer of Hope

Just four games into the regular season on October 17, 1995, Ronald Corey called a press conference at the Montréal Forum and made an announcement that shocked the entire hockey world. Just a few days earlier, Corey had fired longtime general manager Serge Savard, his assistant André Boudrias and head coach Jacques Demers. His first statement to the media concerning the breaking news: "I'll get right to it. It's important that we get the right people."

The media had four days to speculate about who would take the empty spaces in one of hockey's most storied and pressure-filled franchises. The people who would lead the Canadiens would have to be shrewd businessmen with keen hockey senses, and they would have to be able to cope with Montréal's high-intensity, high-pressure environment. Several high-profile names around the league were tossed about in the media, but no one was ready for what Ronald Corey had in mind.

Former Canadien Réjean Houle was named general manager, along with Mario Tremblay as head coach and Yvan Cournoyer as assistant coach. Réjean Houle was promoted from his public-relations job with Molson Breweries to one of the most powerful positions in the organization, his only experience in hockey coming from the days when he wore a Habs jersey. Tremblay gladly left his job in the broadcast booth to replace Demers as the Canadiens bench boss without having ever coached or held any position in hockey other than during his playing days. Tremblay's reply to the many skeptics: "But I have played for many great coaches!"

The first game with the new coaches and managers behind the team seemed to prove to the media that Corey had done the right thing. Tremblay's first test as coach of the Canadiens came against the Maple Leafs. Seated directly behind the bench was president Ronald Corey, hovering above his new coach and watching every move intently. The Canadiens managed a last-minute 3–2 victory, much Mario Tremblay's delight. Showing no professionalism whatsoever, Tremblay high-fived Corey and his players as if to say: "Ha! See, I told you I could coach!"

For the next few months under Tremblay, the Canadiens played good hockey, posting a winning record. But there were rumours circling that behind the dressing-room door, all was not well in Habs land.

When Mario Tremblay was a player with the Canadiens, he was well known for his physical and aggressive style, and when he joined the Canadiens as a coach, he tried to bring that style into the dressing room. He was the coach now, and it was going to be his way or no way at all. The problem was that the Canadiens had a few players with personalities as large as his, and when they combined, it was just a matter of time before things blew up.

Patrick Roy had never been known to keep quiet when he saw something he didn't like or didn't agree with. On a few occasions, Roy and Tremblay had some minor disagreements on the day-to-day running of the team and Roy's place within that system. The clash of two strong wills finally exploded on December 2, 1995, and the aftermath of that day would change the fate of the Canadiens for the next few years.

During a game against the Detroit Red Wings at the Montréal Forum (it seems a lot of unforgettable moments in Habs history have involved the Red Wings in some manner), Patrick Roy was not having any luck stopping the puck. After a few easy goals, fans got under Roy's skin when they started sarcastically cheering every time he made a save.

Under normal circumstances, a coach will pull his goaltender when he has let in several "soft" goals, but Tremblay was out to prove a lesson to his star netminder and left him in for an embarrassing 9 Red Wings goals. Tremblay finally pulled Roy in favour of backup goaltender Pat Jablonski.

Roy casually removed his helmet, put a towel around his neck and brushed by Tremblay on his way to his spot on the bench. He paused as if to think about his next move for just half a second, then turned, gave Tremblay the coldest stare on his way over to Ronald Corey, who was seated just behind the bench, and said in a matter-of-fact voice: "That's the last time I played for Montréal."

The ultimatum had been given. Ronald Corey would have to choose between his coaching staff or his star player. For Corey, the decision was clear. Just four days later, general manager Réjean Houle announced that Patrick Roy had been traded to the Colorado Avalanche along with Mike Keane in return for young goaltender Jocelyn Thibault and forwards Martin Rucinsky and Andrei Kovalenko.

Roy later regretted the way he ended his career with the Canadiens and apologized to Corey for the public outburst—conveniently leaving Tremblay and Houle out of his sympathies.

During his first game against the Canadiens in Colorado, after his new team won the game, Roy scooped up the game puck and flipped it to Tremblay on the Montréal bench. Not a classy move on Roy's part, but he got his point across. Roy went on to win another two Stanley Cups with the Avalanche before retiring with the most successful winning record in hockey history.

The Canadiens didn't fare too badly the rest of the season, finishing with 90 points but unfortunately losing in the first round of the playoffs to the New York Rangers. The next season didn't get any easier for the rookie coach as his tough, in-your-face, my-way-or-the-highway attitude didn't sit well with the players, making Tremblay an outsider on his own team. The Canadiens finished the season with only 77 points and a first-round exit from the playoffs after a five-game series loss to the New Jersey Devils.

Four days after the loss to the Devils, Mario Tremblay called a press conference and, to no one's surprise, announced he was leaving his position as head coach.

His replacement, Alain Vigneault, helped the Canadiens get their focus back in the 1997–98 season, but after two difficult years under the watch of Tremblay, the team was lacking the chemistry that makes a winner, and injuries to their key players kept popping up at the wrong time. Although the Montréal Canadiens made it past the Pittsburgh Penguins in the first round of the playoffs, the Buffalo Sabres swept the Habs out of contention in the conference semifinals.

During the regular season that year, the organization received some bad news. The Canadiens' greatest player, Maurice "the Rocket" Richard, was suffering from cancer. With his usual tough exterior, the Rocket refused to talk about his illness and promised to fight till the end. But it was not all bad news for the Habs legend. After a lengthy campaign to the National Hockey League headquarters by journalist Tom Lapointe, Québec personality Julie Snyder and legions of Maurice Richard supporters, the league finally accepted their proposal to have a trophy named in Richard's honour to be given each year to the player who scores the most goals during the regular season. In the toughest battle of his life, the Rocket fought the disease for another year. But at the age of 78, Maurice Richard had little fight left in him, and on May 22, 2000, he died peacefully in a Montréal hospital.

Although Maurice Richard hadn't played a game of hockey since 1960, some 115,000 people turned out to pay their respects as his body lay in state at the Bell Centre. He was a hero to many while he played the game, and he remains a legend even after his death.

For the Canadiens, things kept getting worse, and they hit their lowest point in 48 years at the end of the 1998–99 regular season. The Habs finished the regular season with a record of 32–39–11 for a total of 75 points, not enough to earn them a spot in the playoffs. Media pressure was intense, but this time, most of it was directed at the management of the team.

In his 17 years as president of the Montréal Canadiens, Ronald Corey had seen his team through some great moments and also some of the worst. With a heavy heart, Corey announced on May 31, 1999, that he was leaving the organization. His replacement was the president of Bauer Nike Hockey, Pierre Boivin, who quickly set about a few changes of his own to get the most storied team in hockey history back on the winning path.

After another bad season that saw the Canadiens out of the playoffs for a second year in a row, Boivin decided to change Corey's management legacy and bring in some new blood and hopefully new life to the team. After a disastrous start to the season and an embarrassing 6–1 loss to the Toronto Maple Leafs before their home crowd, Pierre Boivin decided it was time to change the club's direction. In one sweeping motion, Alain Vigneault and Réjean Houle were fired and replaced by Michel Therrien and André Savard. The new staff made a few important changes to the Canadiens lineup over the summer and by the 2001–02 season, things were finally looking up for the Canadiens after several years of uncertainty. They made a decent run in the playoffs, beating the Boston Bruins in one of the Canadiens' most exciting series in recent years, but lost to the Carolina Hurricanes in six games in the next round. The Canadiens' new goaltending hope for the future, José Theodore, beat out Patrick Roy for the Hart Trophy and added the Vézina and Roger Crozier trophies to his collection that year. Canadiens captain Saku Koivu took home the Bill Masterson Trophy for showing his dedication to the game after battling back from cancer to lead his team into the playoffs.

It was a wave of new hope that the Canadiens were hoping to ride into the 2002–03 season, but the team's losing ways continued. Halfway through the season, with the Canadiens hovering near the bottom of the league, André Savard fired Therrien, the coach he hired only two years earlier, and replaced him with minor-league coach Claude Julien. But the shakeup did little to motivate the Canadiens, and for the fourth time in five years, they missed the playoffs after finishing in 10th place in the eastern standings.

There was a lack of unity on the team despite some quality players, and in order to bring some respect back to the organization, club president Pierre Boivin made the decision on June 2, 2003, to bring back former Canadiens player Bob Gainey as general manager. After spending close to 12 years with the Minnesota/Dallas Stars organization as coach and as general manager, Gainey hoped to return the Canadiens to a place in the league where all fans of the team could lift their heads after years of uncertainty and cheer proudly for *"Les Glorieux!"*

The Canadiens had a respectable 2003–04 season, finishing with 93 points. They met their old playoff archrivals, the Boston Bruins, in the first round and seemed ready to bow out early once again after the Bruins went up in the series three games to the Canadiens' one. Down but not out, the Canadiens frustrated the Bruins at every turn and Theodore managed to keep enough pucks out of the net to let the Canadiens come back and win the series in game seven. Unfortunately for the Habs, they ran into the eventual Stanley Cup winners, the Tampa Bay Lightning, in the next round and were swept in four games.

After a bad start to the 2005–06 season, Gainey had had enough of the inconsistent play of the team and how coach Julien was managing his players. In January, Gainey announced that he was taking the job as interim head coach and that former Canadiens captain Guy Carbonneau would replace him at the start of the 2006–07 season. Under coach Gainey, the Canadiens fared well for the rest of the season, just making it into the playoffs.

They gave their first-round opponents, the Carolina Hurricanes, a scare, winning the first two games in Carolina, but the 'Canes came back and won four straight to eliminate the Canadiens.

However, the future no longer looks so dim for the Canadiens. After several turbulent years in Montréal, goaltender José Theodore was traded to the Colorado Avalanche and ceded his position to backup goaltender Cristobal Huet, who surprised everyone and almost single-handedly won the remaining games in the 2006 season to get the Canadiens into the playoffs. The Canadiens are also relying on young talent such as Thomas Plekanec, Michael Ryder, Christopher Higgins and draft hope Guillaume Latendresse to take the team into the future and bring the pride back to the *bleu, blanc, rouge.*

Appendix I

The Many Homes of the Montréal Canadiens

In the hearts of all true Montréal Canadiens fans, the only real home of the team has always been and will always be the Montréal Forum. But the history of the Canadiens is a lot longer than the history of the Forum, and the team has inhabited its fair share of buildings over the years. From 1909 to the present, they have occupied five different arenas.

Jubilee Rink: The first home of the Canadiens was located on the eastern side of the island of Montréal in what was known as the Hochelaga district. At the time, the Jubilee Rink was a state-of-the-art building that could seat about 3000 people, had two dressing rooms for the teams, a restaurant and space for a band to entertain the crowds during a stoppage of play. The Canadiens' first franchise game was played under the Jubilee roof against the Cobalt Silver Kings, a game the Canadiens won by a score of 7–6. The Canadiens did not stay at the Jubilee

Rink long, preferring the much larger and more centrally located Westmount Arena.

Westmount Arena: It was at this arena, on the corner of Ste. Catherine and Wood streets in Westmount (the city's poshest neighbourhood) that the Canadiens won their first Stanley Cup against the Portland Rosebuds. The Canadiens shared the arena with the Montréal Wanderers for several seasons before it burned down in 1918 and the team was forced to return to the Jubilee Rink until something better could be found. Only two years later, after playing in their first few seasons in the new National Hockey League before crowds as small as 3000, the Canadiens upgraded to the Mount Royal Arena in the Plateau district of Montréal, on Mont Royal Avenue and St. Urbain Street. (That corner is now the site of a Provigo grocery store.)

Mount Royal Arena: The Mount Royal Arena was big, loud and popular with fans, but there was only one problem. It didn't have artificially cooled ice. Despite this setback, the Canadiens played their first game in the arena against the Toronto St. Patricks and defeated them by a score of 14-7. Newsy Lalonde's 6-goal performance sent the packed arena crowd into a frenzy, and about 1000 more people were outside trying to get in to cheer on their favourite team. As the years went on and the Canadiens became more and more popular with the people of Montréal, the organization needed a bigger venue to house all the fans who wanted to see the Habs play. Plus, it became urgent for the team to have a reliable ice surface on which to play when the 1924 season started on November 29 and the ice was not yet ready. Even though they were locked into a contract with the Mount Royal Arena, the Canadiens decided to make the Montréal Forum the site of their first game of that season. Billy Boucher scored a hat trick against the Toronto St. Pats to help the Canadiens to a 7–1 victory.

The Montréal Forum: The Montréal Forum, on Ste. Catherine Street and Atwater Avenue in the city's downtown, was originally intended to be the permanent home of the new Montréal Maroons, but the Canadiens organization coveted the venue's ample seating and modern facilities and moved in permanently in 1926. The Forum was not the specific domain of the Canadiens, however. They shared the building with hated rivals the Maroons until 1938, when financial troubles forced the Maroons to withdraw from the league. During that time, the Forum was the site of some of the most intense matchups between the two Montréal teams, the likes of which have not been seen since. With francophone Montréal cheering for the Canadiens and anglophone Montréal cheering for the Maroons, the Forum was always full of excitement, emotion and violence, both on the ice and off. Police were regular visitors to Montréal games involving both teams, more often to break up fights in the stands than battles on the ice.

The Montréal Forum, the most recognized and most celebrated temple of hockey in National Hockey League history, saw the Montréal Canadiens through 22 of their 24 Stanley Cups, witnessed the performances of some of the sport's greatest stars and was the site of some of the most important moments in the history of the city. Howie Morenz first got the crowds of the Montréal Forum to their feet with his amazing ability to score goals, and he also brought them to tears when he passed away in 1937 and his body lay in state at centre ice. It was also the site where another Montréal Canadiens legend brought the entire city to its feet, cheering every goal scored by the city's favourite son, Maurice Richard. He was a hero everyone could believe in, and when he was suspended for the remainder of the season in 1955, the Forum was where the city united in anger at those trying to keep their hero down. Jean Béliveau, "Boom Boom" Geoffrion, Doug Harvey, Jacques Plante, Elmer Lach, Toe Blake, Frank Selke, Dick Irvin, Yvan Cournoyer, Guy Lafleur, Ken Dryden, Bob Gainey, Patrick Roy: all names that made the Montréal Forum the centre of the city for 70 years.

During those 70 years, the Forum underwent some major renovations (in 1949 and 1968) to accommodate increasing crowds and bring in more revenue. But as the years went on and the Canadiens organization continued to expand, the Habs were forced to start looking for a new home. It would have been too costly to undertake a major refitting of the old Forum, so Canadiens president Ronald Corey chose an empty lot in Montréal's downtown area, near all amenities, to build the future home of the Montréal Canadiens.

The Bell Centre: Construction on the new building began in 1995, and it would be ready to host the team near the end of the season. On March 15, 1996, a ceremony was held to celebrate the new building, which at the time was called the Molson Centre. Canadiens alumni were brought out in force to bring good luck to the new building, and none received a warmer welcome than Maurice Richard, who received a standing ovation for more than five minutes. Fighting back tears, the Rocket took in every moment he could, savouring the cheers that reminded him of when he used to proudly wear the Canadiens jersey.

"I closed my eyes and it brought me back to my younger days," the aging superstar said of that night.

With its new luxury boxes and sophisticated technology, the Bell Centre can seat as many as 23,000 people. It is truly a modern building for the modern game of hockey, but for those who remember the Montréal Forum, the Bell Centre will never have the same feeling and history. But as long as the fans keep coming and (hopefully) the Habs keep winning, perhaps the ghosts of the old Forum will return and find a new home in the Bell Centre.

Appendix II

The Stats

After almost a century in existence, the Montréal Canadiens have picked up some of the most impressive team and individual statistics in National Hockey League history. Here are just a few from their glorious past.

Legend

GP – Games Played	PIM – Penalty in Minutes
W – Wins	SF – Semifinal
L – Loses	QF – Quarterfinal
T – Ties	PR – Preliminary Round
OT – Overtime	DSF – Division Semifinal
GF – Goals For	CF – Conference Final
GA – Goals Against	CQF – Conference Quarter Final
Pts – Points	CSF – Conference Semifinal

Scoring Leaders

Player	Games Played	Goals	Assists	Points
Guy Lafleur	961	518	**728**	**1246**
Jean Béliveau	1125	507	712	1219
Henri Richard	**1256**	358	688	1046
Maurice Richard	978	**544**	421	965
Larry Robinson	1202	197	686	883
Yvan Cournoyer	968	428	435	863
Jacques Lemaire	853	366	469	835
Steve Shutt	871	408	368	776
Bernie Geoffrion	766	371	388	759
Elmer Lach	664	215	408	623

Season by Season Record in the National Hockey League

Season	GP	W	L	T	OT	GF	GA	Pts	PIM
1917–18	22	13	9	0		115	84	26	
1918–19	18	10	8	0		88	78	20	257
1919–20	24	13	11	0		129	113	26	221
1920–21	24	13	11	0		112	99	26	315
1921–22	24	12	11	1		88	94	25	174
1922–23	24	13	9	2		73	61	28	174
1923–24	24	13	11	0		59	48	26	144
1924–25	30	17	11	2		93	56	36	371
1925–26	36	11	24	1		79	108	23	458
1926–27	44	28	14	2		99	67	58	395
1927–28	44	26	11	7		116	48	59	496
1928–29	44	22	7	15		71	43	59	465
1929–30	44	21	14	9		142	114	51	600
1930–31	44	26	10	8		129	89	60	602
1931–32	48	25	16	7		128	111	57	450
1932–33	48	18	25	5		92	115	41	468
1933–34	48	22	20	6		99	101	50	308
1934–35	48	19	23	6		110	145	44	314
1935–36	48	11	26	11		82	123	33	317
1936–37	48	24	18	6		115	111	54	298
1937–38	48	18	17	13		123	128	49	340
1938–39	48	15	24	9		115	146	39	294
1939–40	48	10	33	5		90	167	25	338
1940–41	48	16	26	6		121	147	38	435
1941–42	48	18	27	3		134	173	39	504
1942–43	50	19	19	12		181	191	50	318
1943–44	50	38	5	7		234	109	83	557
1944–45	50	38	8	4		228	121	80	376
1945–46	50	28	17	5		172	134	61	337
1946–47	60	34	16	10		189	138	78	561

Season by Season Record in the National Hockey League (continued)

Season	GP	W	L	T	OT	GF	GA	Pts	PIM
1947–48	60	20	29	11		147	169	51	724
1948–49	60	28	23	9		152	126	65	782
1949–50	70	29	22	19		172	150	77	736
1950–51	70	25	30	15		173	184	65	835
1951–52	70	34	26	10		195	164	78	661
1952–53	70	28	23	19		155	148	75	777
1953–54	70	35	24	11		195	141	81	1064
1954–55	70	41	18	11		228	157	93	890
1955–56	70	45	15	10		222	131	100	977
1956–57	70	35	23	12		210	155	82	870
1957–58	70	43	17	10		250	158	96	945
1958–59	70	39	18	13		258	158	91	760
1959–60	70	40	18	12		255	178	92	756
1960–61	70	41	19	10		254	188	92	811
1961–62	70	42	14	14		259	166	98	818
1962–63	70	28	19	23		225	183	79	751
1963–64	70	36	21	13		209	167	85	982
1964–65	70	36	23	11		211	185	83	1033
1965–66	70	41	21	8		239	173	90	884
1966–67	70	32	25	13		202	188	77	879
1967–68	74	42	22	10		236	167	94	700
1968–69	76	46	19	11		271	202	103	780
1969–70	76	38	22	16		244	201	92	892
1970–71	78	42	23	13		291	216	97	1271
1971–72	78	46	16	16		307	205	108	783
1972–73	78	52	10	16		329	184	120	783
1973–74	78	45	24	9		293	240	99	761
1974–75	80	47	14	19		374	225	113	155
1975–76	80	58	11	11		337	174	127	977
1976–77	80	60	8	12		387	171	132	764
1977–78	80	59	10	11		359	183	129	745
1978–79	80	52	17	11		337	204	115	803

Season by Season Record in the National Hockey League (continued)

Season	GP	W	L	T	OT	GF	GA	Pts	PIM
1979–80	80	47	20	13		328	240	107	874
1980–81	80	45	22	13		332	232	103	1398
1981–82	80	46	17	17		360	223	109	1463
1982–83	80	42	24	14		350	286	98	1116
1983–84	80	35	40	5		286	295	75	1371
1984–85	80	41	27	12		309	262	94	1464
1985–86	80	40	33	7		330	280	87	1372
1986–87	80	41	29	10		277	241	92	1802
1987–88	80	45	22	13		298	238	103	1830
1988–89	80	53	18	9		315	218	115	1537
1989–90	80	41	28	11		288	234	93	1590
1990–91	80	39	30	11		273	249	89	1425
1991–92	80	41	28	11		267	207	93	1556
1992–93	84	48	30	6		326	280	102	1788
1993–94	84	41	29	14		283	248	96	1524
1994–95	48	18	23	7		125	148	43	840
1995–96	82	40	32	10		265	248	90	1847
1996–97	82	31	36	15		249	276	77	1469
1997–98	82	37	32	13		235	208	87	1547
1998–99	82	32	39	11		184	209	75	1299
1999–00	82	35	34	9	4	196	194	83	1067
2000–01	82	28	40	8	6	206	232	70	1020
2001–02	82	36	31	12	3	207	209	87	974
2002–03	82	30	35	8	9	206	234	77	900
2003–04	82	41	30	7	4	208	192	93	1039
2005–06	82	42	31	—	9	243	247	93	1312
Grand Totals	**5628**	**2891**	**1865**	**837**	**35**	**18528**	**15033**	**6654**	**72660**

Season and Playoff Record

Season	Regular Season Finish	Playoffs
1917–18	1st in NHL (tie)	Lost NHL final vs. Toronto
1918–19	2nd in NHL	Reached final, No Decision
1919–20	2nd in NHL	Out of playoffs
1920–21	3rd in NHL	Out of playoffs
1921–22	3rd in NHL	Missed Playoffs
1922–23	2nd in NHL	Lost NHL final vs. Ottawa
1923–24	2nd in NHL	**Stanley Cup Champion**
1924–25	3rd in NHL	Lost final vs. Victoria
1925–26	7th (last) in NHL	Out of playoffs
1926–27	2nd in Canadian	Lost SF vs. Ottawa
1927–28	1st in Canadian	Lost SF vs. Mtl. Maroons
1928–29	1st in Canadian	Lost SF vs. Boston
1929–30	2nd in Canadian	**Stanley Cup Champion**
1930–31	1st in Canadian	**Stanley Cup Champion**
1931–32	1st in Canadian	Lost SF vs. NY Rangers
1932–33	3rd in Canadian	Lost QF vs. NY Rangers
1933–34	2nd in Canadian	Lost QF vs. Chicago
1934–35	3rd in Canadian	Lost QF vs. NY Rangers
1935–36	4th (last) in Canadian	Out of playoffs
1936–37	1st in Canadian	Lost SF vs. Detroit
1937–38	3rd in Canadian	Lost QF vs. Chicago
1938–39	6th in NHL	Lost QF vs. Detroit
1939–40	7th (last) in NHL	Out of playoffs
1940–41	6th in NHL	Lost QF vs. Chicago
1941–42	6th in NHL	Lost QF vs. Detroit
1942–43	4th in NHL	Lost SF vs. Boston
1943–44	1st in NHL	**Stanley Cup Champion**
1944–45	1st in NHL	Lost SF vs. Toronto
1945–46	1st in NHL	**Stanley Cup Champion**
1946–47	1st in NHL	Lost final vs. Toronto
1947–48	5th in NHL	Out of playoffs
1948–49	3rd in NHL	Lost SF vs. Detroit
1949–50	2nd in NHL	Lost SF vs. NY Rangers

Season and Playoff Record (continued)

Season	Regular Season Finish	Playoffs
1950–51	3rd in NHL	Lost final vs. Toronto
1951–52	2nd in NHL	Lost final vs. Detroit
1952–53	2nd in NHL	**Stanley Cup Champion**
1953–54	2nd in NHL	Lost final vs. Detroit
1954–55	2nd in NHL	Lost final vs. Detroit
1955–56	1st in NHL	**Stanley Cup Champion**
1956–57	2nd in NHL	**Stanley Cup Champion**
1957–58	1st in NHL	**Stanley Cup Champion**
1958–59	1st in NHL	**Stanley Cup Champion**
1959–60	1st in NHL	**Stanley Cup Champion**
1960–61	1st in NHL	Lost SF vs. Chicago
1961–62	1st in NHL	Lost SF vs. Chicago
1962–63	3rd in NHL	Lost SF vs. Toronto
1963–64	1st in NHL	Lost SF vs. Toronto
1964–65	2nd in NHL	**Stanley Cup Champion**
1965–66	1st in NHL	**Stanley Cup Champion**
1966–67	2nd in NHL	Lost final vs. Toronto
1967–68	1st in East	**Stanley Cup Champion**
1968–69	1st in East	**Stanley Cup Champion**
1969–70	5th in East	Out of playoffs
1970–71	3rd in East	**Stanley Cup Champion**
1971–72	3rd in East	Lost QF vs. NYR
1972–73	1st in East	**Stanley Cup Champion**
1973–74	2nd in East	Lost QF vs. NYR
1974–75	1st in Norris	Lost SF vs. Buffalo
1975–76	1st in Norris	**Stanley Cup Champion**
1976–77	1st in Norris	**Stanley Cup Champion**
1977–78	1st in Norris	**Stanley Cup Champion**
1978–79	1st in Norris	**Stanley Cup Champion**
1979–80	1st in Norris	Lost QF vs. Minnesota
1980–81	1st in Norris	Lost PR vs. Edmonton

Season and Playoff Record (continued)

Season	Regular Season Finish	Playoffs
1981–82	1st in Norris	Lost DSF vs. Québec
1982–83	2nd in Adams	Lost DSF vs. Buffalo
1983–84	4th in Adams	Lost CF vs. NY Islanders
1984–85	1st in Adams	Lost DF vs. Québec
1985–86	2nd in Adams	**Stanley Cup Champion**
1986–87	2nd in Adams	Lost CF vs. Philadelphia
1987–88	1st in Adams	Lost DF vs. Boston
1988–89	1st in Adams	Lost final vs. Calgary
1989–90	3rd in Adams	Lost DF vs. Boston
1990–91	2nd in Adams	Lost DF vs. Boston
1991–92	1st in Adams	Lost DF vs. Boston
1992–93	3rd in Adams	**Stanley Cup Champion**
1993–94	3rd in Northeast	Lost CQF vs. Boston
1994–95	6th in Northeast	Out of playoffs
1995–96	3rd in Northeast	Lost CQF vs. NY Rangers
1996–97	4th in Northeast	Lost CQF vs. New Jersey
1997–98	4th in Northeast	Lost CSF vs. Buffalo
1998–99	5th (last) in Northeast	Out of playoffs
1999–00	4th in Northeast	Out of playoffs
2000–01	5th (last) in Northeast	Out of playoffs
2001–02	4th in Northeast	Lost CSF vs. Carolina
2002–03	4th in Northeast	Out of playoffs
2003–04	4th in Northeast	Lost CSF vs. Tampa Bay
2005–06	3rd in Northeast	Lost CQF vs. Carolina

Players named to the Hockey Hall of Fame

1945 – Howie Morenz, Georges Vézina
1947 – Aurèle Joliat
1950 – Newsy Lalonde, Joe Malone
1958 – Sprague Cleghorn, Herb Gardiner
1960 – Sylvio Mantha
1961 – Joe Hall, Georges Hainsworth, Maurice Richard
1962 – Jack Laviolette, Didier Pitre
1964 – Bill Durnan, Babe Siebert
1966 – Toe Blake, Emile Bouchard, Elmer Lach, Ken Reardon
1970 – Tom Johnson
1972 – Jean Béliveau, Bernard Geoffrion
1973 – Doug Harvey
1974 – Dickie Moore
1978 – Jacques Plante
1979 – Henri Richard
1980 – Lorne Worsley
1981 – Frank Mahovlich
1982 – Yvan Cournoyer
1983 – Ken Dryden
1984 – Jacques Lemaire
1985 – Bert Olmstead
1986 – Serge Savard
1987 – Jacques Laperrière
1988 – Guy Lafleur, Buddy O'Connor
1992 – Bob Gainey
1993 – Guy Lapointe, Steve Shutt
1995 – Larry Robinson
2000 – Denis Savard

Builders in the Hall of Fame

1945 – William Northey
1958 – Donat Raymond
1960 – Frank J. Selke
1962 – John Ambrose O'Brien
1963 – Leo Dandurand, Tommy Gorman
1973 – Hartland de Montarville Molson
1977 – Jos Cattarinich
1978 – Sam Pollock
1991 – Scotty Bowman

Numbers Retired by the Montréal Canadiens

Jersey Number 1: Jacques Plante played for the Canadiens from 1952 to 1963. In 556 games, he recorded 314 wins and only 133 losses with a goals against average of 2.23. His number was officially retired in 1995.

Jersey Number 2: Doug Harvey played for the Canadiens from 1948 to 1961. He was the team's best defenceman, playing in 890 games with the Canadiens, scoring 76 goals and 371 assists for a total of 447 points. His number was officially retired in 1995.

Jersey Number 4: Jean Béliveau played his entire career with the Montréal Canadiens, from 1951 to 1971. He scored 507 goals and 712 assists in 1125 games. He won 10 Stanley Cups with the team. His number was retired in 1971.

Jersey Number 5: Bernard "Boom Boom" Geoffrion was with the Canadiens from 1950 to 1964. He scored 371 goals as a Montréal Canadien and won six Stanley Cups with the team. His number was retired in 2006.

Jersey Number 7: Howie Morenz was the first Canadiens to have his number retired by the team. He won three Stanley Cups with the organization and was the heart and soul of the team until his death in 1937. His number was retired in 1937.

Jersey Number 9: Maurice "the Rocket" Richard played his entire career with the Montréal Canadiens and is the franchise's most popular and celebrated player. He scored the most goals in team history, with 544. His number was retired in 1960.

Jersey Number 10: Guy Lafleur is the leading scorer in Montréal Canadiens history. He led the Canadiens to five Stanley Cups. His number was retired in 1985.

Jersey Number 12: Dickie Moore and Yvan Cournoyer: both natural goal scorers, both were a large part of the Canadiens' success during their time. Their numbers were retired in a ceremony in late 2005.

Jersey Number 16: Henri "Pocket Rocket" Richard played his entire career with the Canadiens and won the most Stanley Cups in league history with 11. He scored 358 goals and 688 assists for a total of 1046 points. His number was retired in 1975.

Single Season Team Records

Most Points: 132 points, 1976–77
Most Wins: 60, 1976–77
Most Losses: 40, 1983–84, 2000–01
Most Goals For: 387, 1976–77
Most Goals Against: 295, 1983–84
Most Penalty Minutes: 1847, 1995–96
Most Shutouts: 22, 1928–29
Longest Undefeated Streak: 28 games from December 18, 1977, to February 23, 1978
Longest Losing Streak: 12 games from February 13, 1926, to March 13, 1926

Individual Team Records

Career

Most Seasons	20	Henri Richard, Jean Béliveau
Most Games	1256	Henri Richard
Most Goals	544	Maurice Richard
Most Assists	728	Guy Lafleur
Most Points	1246	Guy Lafleur
Most Penalty Minutes	2248	Chris Nilan
Most Shutouts	75	Georges Hainsworth
Most Consecutive Games Played	560	Doug Jarvis

Single Season

Most Points	136	Guy Lafleur 1976–77
Most Goals	60	Steve Shutt 1976–77, Guy Lafleur 1977–78
Most Assists	82	Pete Mahovlich 1974–75
Most Penalty Minutes	358	Chris Nilan 1984–85
Most Points by a defenceman	85	Larry Robinson 1976–77
Most Shutouts	22	Georges Hainsworth

Single Game

Most Points	8	Maurice Richard (December 28, 1944) and Bert Olmstead (January 9, 1954)
Most Goals	6	Newsy Lalonde (January 10, 1920)
Most Assists	6	Elmer Lach (February 6, 1943)

Notes on Sources

Allen, Kevin, and Bob Duff. *Without Fear: Hockey's 50 Greatest Goaltenders.* Chicago: Triumph Books, 2002.

Brown, William. *The Montréal Maroons: The Forgotten Stanley Cup Champions.* Montréal: Vehicule Press, 1999.

Bruneau, Pierre, and Leandre Normand. *La Glorieuse Histoire des Canadiens.* Montréal: Les Éditions de l'Homme, 2003.

Carrier, Roch. *Our Life With the Rocket: The Maurice Richard Story.* Toronto: Viking Press, 2001.

Coleman, Charles L. *The Trail of the Stanley Cup.* Volumes 1, 2, 3. Sherbrooke: National Hockey League, 1969.

Diamond, Dan, ed. *Total Hockey.* New York: Total Sports Publishing, 1998

Diamond, Dan, ed. *Total NHL.* Toronto: Dan Diamond and Associates, 2003

Cox, Damien, and Gord Stellick. *'67: The Maple Leafs, their Sensational Victory and the End of an Empire.* Toronto: Wiley, 2004.

Dryden, Ken. *The Game.* Canada: Wiley, 2005.

Goyens, Chrys, et al. *The Montréal Forum: Forever Proud.* Montréal: Les Éditions Felix, 1996.

Goyens, Chrys, and Allan Turowetz. *Lions in Winter.* Scarborough: Prentice-Hall, 1986.

Leonetti, Mike. *Canadiens Legends: Montréal's Hockey Heroes.* Vancouver: Raincoast Books, 2003.

Irvin, Dick. *The Habs: An Oral History from 1940-1980.* Toronto: McClelland & Stewart Inc., 1991.

Liss, Howard. *Goal: Hockey's Stanley Cup Playoffs.* New York: Delacourt Press, 1970.

McFarlane, Brian. *The Habs.* Toronto: Stoddart Press, 1996.

Mouton, Claude. *The Montréal Canadiens.* Toronto: Key Porter Books, 1987.

Richard, Maurice and Fischler, Stan. *The Flying Frenchmen: Hockey's Greatest Dynasty.* New York: Hawthorn Books Inc., 1971.

J. Alexander Poulton

J. Alexander Poulton is a writer, photographer and genuine enthusiast of Canada's national pastime. A resident of Montréal all his life, he has developed a healthy passion for hockey ever since he saw his first Montréal Canadiens game. His favourite memory was meeting the legendary gentleman hockey player Jean Beliveau, who in 1988 towered over the young awe-struck author.

He earned his B.A. in English Literature from McGill University and his graduate diploma in Journalism from Concordia University. He has four other books to his credit: *Canadian Hockey Record Breakers, Greatest Moments in Canadian Hockey, World's Greatest Soccer Players* and *Greatest Games of the Stanley Cup.*

OverTime Books

If you enjoyed *The Montréal Canadiens*, be sure to check out these other great titles from OverTime Books:

NEW FOR FALL 2006

THE EDMONTON OILERS

by Peter Boer

Take a look at the winningest expansion team in the history of the NHL. Since 1972, the Edmonton Oilers have been on a roller coaster, enjoying one Stanley Cup victory after another followed by many seasons out of the playoffs. Here is the story of the team that helped make Edmonton the City of Champions.

Softcover • 5.25" X 8.25" • 168 pages • ISBN10 1-897277-02-4 • ISBN13 978-1897277-02-7• $9.95

NHL ENFORCERS:
The Rough and Tough Guys of Hockey

by Arpon Basu

Throughout the history of professional hockey, the tough guys of the game have done much to define hockey, both for better and for worse. Read about enforcers such as Eddie Shore, Tie Domi, "Tiger" Williams, Bob Probert and so many more.

Softcover • 5.25" X 8.25" • 168 pages • ISBN10 1-897277-10-5 • ISBN13 978-1897277-10-2 • $9.95

GREATEST STANLEY CUP VICTORIES:
The Battles and the Rivalries

by J. Alexander Poulton

A look back at some of the NHL's most memorable battles for hockey supremacy.

Softcover • 5.25" X 8.25" • 168 pages • ISBN10 1-897277-06-7 • ISBN13 978-1897277-06-5 • $9.95

HOCKEY'S HOTTEST PLAYERS:
The On- & Off-Ice Stories of the Superstars

by Arpon Basu

Sports journalist Arpon Basu profiles today's rising stars in the National Hockey League. He looks not only at their on-ice performance and statistics but also probes the human story behind their victories and struggles, revealing the journey they've taken to reach the highest echelons of their sport.

Softcover • 5.25" X 8.25" • 144 pages • ISBN10 0-9737681-3-4 • ISBN13 978-0-9737681-3-8 • $9.95

CANADIAN HOCKEY TRIVIA:
The Facts, Stats and Strange Tales of Canadian Hockey

by J. Alexander Poulton

Hockey is so much a part of Canadian life that the theme song to *Hockey Night in Canada* has been called our unofficial national anthem. Read the fascinating facts from Canada's favorite game such as the almost-forgotten Winnipeg Falcons, who were the first Canadian team to win Olympic gold in 1920, and Dennis O'Brien, who holds the record for most NHL teams played in a single season.

Softcover • 5.25" X 8.25" • 168 pages • ISBN10 1-897277-01-6 • ISBN13 978-1-897277-01-0 • $9.95

Lone Pine Publishing is the exclusive distributor for OverTime Books.
If you cannot find these titles at your local bookstore, contact us:
Canada: 1-800-661-9017 USA: 1-800-518-3541.